Being
Martha

Being
Martha

The Inside Story of Martha Stewart and Her Amazing Life

LLOYD ALLEN

WILEY

John Wiley & Sons, Inc.

Published by John Wiley & Sons, Inc., Hoboken, New Jersey
Published simultaneously in Canada

Design and composition by Navta Associates, Inc.

For general information about our other products and services, please contact our Customer Care Department within the United States at (800) 762-2974, outside the United States at (317) 572-3993 or fax (317) 572-4002.

Wiley also publishes its books in a variety of electronic formats. Some content that appears in print may not be available in electronic books. For more information about Wiley products, visit our web site at www.wiley.com.

Library of Congress Cataloging-in-Publication Data:

Allen, Lloyd.
    Being Martha : the inside story of Martha Stewart and her amazing life/ Lloyd Allen.
        p. cm.
    ISBN-13 978-0-471-77101-2 (cloth : alk. paper)
    ISBN-10 0-471-77101-5 (cloth : alk. paper)
    1. Stewart, Martha. 2. Home economists—United States—Biography. 3. Business-women—United States—Biography. I. Title.
TX140.S74A66 2006
338.7'6164092—dc22
[B]

2005025141

Printed in the United States of America

10 9 8 7 6 5 4 3 2 1

For Sam and Phoebe

Contents

Acknowledgments

I am a friend and fan of Martha Stewart's who wanted to tell what I know of her. I could not have done this without the help and support of many people.

I have to thank Martha for trusting me and allowing me unfettered entrée to people in her life who know the truth about this complex woman's personality and who would not have come forward without her approval and cooperation.

I owe Martha's daughter, Alexis, untold gratitude for her insight and her saintly patience over the past two years. Her guidance and approving glances lightened my burden, but most of all it was her smile and sense of humor that made it all worth it.

Sitting and talking with Martha's mother—what can I say? She's seen it all. I enjoyed her stories, and she was just a lot of fun to be with (despite the occasional fracas coming from the songbirds). Without George and Laura's memories the book would not be half of what it is, for they are the two siblings closest to Martha who worked beside their sister to help her realize the giant dream.

And to everyone else who allowed me into their memories of Martha—you know I can't thank you enough. In no particular order, I have to thank Audrey Doneger, Beverly Feldman, Brooke Dojny, Charles Case, Corey Tippin, Eva Scrivo, John Hanson Jr., Judy Morris, Lisa Wagner, Louise Felix, Necy Fernandez, Omar Honeyman, Sarah Gross, and Victoria Sloat. If I thought I knew who Martha was, each and every one of you showed me that she was so much more than I could have ever believed.

There were those who said no one wanted to hear the other side of the Martha story—that the public doesn't buy anything unless it involves gossip and tawdry tales. So thanks to Gerry Gross, who thought differently and introduced me to my agent, Jill Kneerim, who delivered me to Tom Miller at Wiley, who is a fan of Martha's and not only believed in the idea for the book but is one hell of a good editor. Many thanks to his assistant, Juliet Grames, for helping input Tom's edits and also for the reference to Shakespeare by virtue of her lovely name.

I love words, I enjoy challenges, and I have dreamed of writing a book, but I am not a journalist. As a first-time author, I could not have done this book without the help of Natasha Stoynoff, who literally played the Sundance Kid to my Butch Cassidy. My hat is off to my writing mentor, who taught me untold tricks; she's a true gunslinger who showed me where to place the dynamite and how to pull the trigger on the run.

To my wife, Leslie, who introduced me to the genius of Martha Stewart nearly thirty years ago—thank you for all your patience and understanding over the past two years and for always believing in me.

Introduction

O f all the stories I've heard about Martha Stewart, my favorite is a seemingly ordinary little moment. Years ago, Martha was visiting her friend Beverly Bronfeld, who owned a tiny antiques shop a few blocks from Martha's home in Westport, Connecticut. The shop was filled with the magic and musty aroma of an old attic. Martha adored it. She would pop in at least once a week and marvel at Beverly's treasures, especially her extensive Fire King Jade-ite collection and porcelain salt and pepper shakers.

"I wonder whose table *these* came from," Martha mused one day, picking up a pair and admiring their delicate silhouettes. "I'd *love* to have seen this person's kitchen!"

As Martha browsed with her daughter, Alexis, or Lexi as she is called, she noticed the pungent scent of onions and garlic. She scanned the room and didn't see any food anywhere, but she did see a side door open a few inches—it led to another room attached to the shop. As Martha followed her nose closer to the door, the scent grew stronger. Without hesitating, she pushed open the door, and there in a small kitchen stood a short man who looked to be in his eighties, stirring a simmering pot of something that smelled intoxicating.

"Oh, that's Mr. Borchetta, my landlord," Beverly rushed over and explained. Martha, with Lexi trailing behind her, had already charged into the man's apartment to where he stood, startled, wooden spoon in hand.

Mr. Borchetta, who was born in Italy, owned the building that housed Beverly's shop, which used to be a grocery store until Beverly started renting it. He still lived in the semiattached apartment next door and loved to cook. He was always emerging from the connecting door with a wooden spoon in hand, asking Beverly to sample his sauce of the day and give her opinion.

"What is *that*?" Martha asked, pointing to his pot. "It smells delicious."

He told her it was *pasta e fagiole* soup. Martha reached over and plucked the wooden spoon out of Mr. Borchetta's hand, dipped it into the simmering pot, and tasted.

"Mmmm. What's giving it that zest? Is that a ham bone I see? Did you soak the beans overnight first?" She dipped the spoon in again. "Lexi, Lexi—come here. You have to try this."

Mr. Borchetta had never met Martha Stewart before and had no idea who this stranger eating his soup was. But one passionate cook always recognizes another, and their kinship was immediate.

The two of them stood in the tiny kitchen for what seemed like an hour as Martha interrogated Mr. Borchetta about his family recipes. What did he make for Easter? For Christmas? For

Thanksgiving? They ran through the list of all the holidays and seasons, with the old man explaining how he basted and sifted and whisked.

When Martha and Lexi finally left, Martha was armed with dozens of new recipes scrawled on the backs of old envelopes.

To me, this simple scene sums up my friend Martha Stewart.

First, she's someone who gets all charged up when she discovers something unique and wonderful, especially when she finds it in the most unlikely of places. One of her special abilities is to spot and appreciate talent and beauty and zest in everyday people and things. This is a woman who will travel to the ends of the earth just to get the best hot dog or egg and bacon sandwich she's ever tasted.

Second, when Martha makes a great find, she wants to share it with the world. You can bet that *pasta e fagiole* recipe—probably one Mr. Borchetta's grandmother used to make—found its way into one of Martha's cookbooks. She wanted any homemaker in North America to be able to have some of Mr. Borchetta's home cooking bubbling over on her stove, too.

The Martha Stewart I know is not the one pundits ranted about on television as I watched one sweltering June day in 2003 in my sister's living room in Texas. Thanks to her digital satellite dish, I was able to hear the indictment in the case of *The United States of America versus Martha Stewart* on five hundred channels. I've known Martha and her family for nearly three decades. At that moment in 2003, not only was I shocked and dumbfounded, I was fed up.

I was exasperated at the stories I had been reading about

Martha in the months and years leading up to this moment. The headlines had screamed about how she yelled at her underlings or how she wanted everything done her way. They claimed she had mood swings, she never slept, she made her family work for her, she was mean to her husband and drove him away, she is an impatient perfectionist who talks down to her audience, she screams at her maids and gardeners and neighbors and waiters and the town authorities and even some little kids along the way. *Just who does she think she is?* was the refrain. Somewhere along the way, the media's portrayal and much of the public's picture of Martha Stewart became a combination of Betty Crocker and Cruella de Vil.

I think that when she was just a former model-turned-broker-turned-housewife-turned-caterer, her success was socially acceptable. As long as she stayed close to homes and gardens, the press and public were willing to embrace her. But as her stock rose and she showed herself as a cutting-edge female business and media mogul who struck ingenious multimillion-dollar deals with the top brass at Kmart and Time Warner, it was time to cut her down. Rich, famous, talented, female, *and* good-looking? No way!

Martha was accused by one writer of taking everyone by the heels and shaking all the money out of them. Actually, Martha was simply a better businessperson than any man she encountered. Rather than being vilified, she should have been commended—but she was a woman. I read horrible headlines about her time and time again. The public lapped up every wild story and rumor whether they were true or not.

.   .   .

In Weston, Connecticut, the town I have lived in for over twenty years, and its sister town, Westport, where I lived around the corner from Martha Stewart for five years, the name *Martha* rolls off everyone's tongues with the familiarity of last night's dessert. Everyone claims to know Martha like they know their own backyards. But do they really?

One day recently I was waiting in a doctor's office in Westport and struck up a conversation with another patient in the waiting room.

"You look tired," she said, after I had yawned for the tenth time.

"Oh, I've been burning the midnight oil. I'm a writer. I'm writing a book on Martha." Of course she knew who I meant. In our town "Martha" is like "Cher": no need for last names. The woman glared.

"I hate her. Are you going to talk to all the people she stole from?"

"Did she steal from you? Do you know her?"

She shook her head. "No, but I've *read* . . ."

That attitude is exactly why I wrote this book. That day in Texas, after I watched the phalanx of press people follow Martha into Manhattan's federal court building to surrender to the authorities, I turned off the television, went out to the front porch, and took a long look at the sky. I decided that my friend had been wronged and misunderstood, and I wanted to help make things right. Yes, she has a temper, is highly ambitious, and has the highest standards for herself and those around her. Are those crimes? She also has other sides: she is compassionate, thoughtful, and inspirational. You rarely hear about those aspects of her personality. I'm here to tell you about them.

This book has been a two-year labor of love that took me inside Martha's world. Martha trusted me enough to allow me to speak to her close friends and family members, and she did not interfere along the way. I went to Turkey Hill, Martha's home made famous on her television show *Martha Stewart Living*, to chat with her mother, Martha Kostyra. I met the Cookie Lady of Westport, whose lemon squares, under Martha's tutelage, became legendary. I sought out Alexis; we took long walks in New York City, through Tribeca and SoHo, as we talked about her mother. I traveled to Alderson Prison on a snowy day and talked to Martha herself in the dingy visitor's room. I talked to the people who *really* know her—the cooks, the stylists, the assistants, the friends, and countless others who were influenced by Martha and were at her side as she built her empire.

I am not a journalist. I went to these people with no clear agenda other than to hear what they had to say about her. I sat in their kitchens, drank their coffee, turned on my iPod recorder, and asked them: *Who is the real Martha Stewart?* My interviews were not about asking leading questions but rather about listening to the people who had something to say about what makes Martha tick.

While my own recollections of Martha may tend toward the warm and fuzzy after being sifted through a filter of friendship—I admit it, I love Martha, warts and all—the others in this book tell the unvarnished truth. Through their eyes, you will see a woman with an inexhaustible inner fire and drive that have made her one of the most successful businesswomen the world has ever seen. You will see a benefactor and a teacher.

Many people in this book view their time with Martha as a turning point in their careers, if not their lives. You'll have a peek at Martha Stewart's carefree and wild side. She's someone who enjoys the smallest things in life with the wonder of a child seeing something for the first time. By the time you finish reading, you will see Martha as a human being who is as imperfect as any other, who makes mistakes, and who is struggling in her own way to connect with others, to love and be loved.

This book gives a fuller portrait than we have seen before of a complicated and fascinating woman. My hope is that by reading this more complete view of Martha you will have a better understanding of who and why she is.

1

Martha and Me

Have a taste.

—MARTHA STEWART

I t was a picture-perfect Martha Stewart moment in June 1977.

As I pulled into the gravel driveway of Martha's home in Westport, Connecticut, for the first time, I caught sight of two pretty young women standing and chatting on an impeccably manicured lawn. At first glance, I thought they must be sisters—young women clad in matching khaki shorts and colorful bikini tops. They looked adorable as they approached the car with their identical long, tanned legs striding in unison. I didn't realize that the taller of the two was Martha Stewart, who at that time was beginning to make a name for herself as a caterer and party planner, until she got closer to the car and introduced herself, then her thirteen-year-old daughter, Alexis.

"Come on in. I'm just taking something out of the oven," she said with a megawatt grin, ushering us into the kitchen, "and you've *got* to taste it."

I was tagging along that day with my then almost-girlfriend and later wife, Leslie Leibman, an artist-designer who was working with Martha as a stylist for the many parties and events she handled and for the photo layouts Martha produced for *House Beautiful* magazine. Martha was known for spotting and putting talented people around her; she had recognized Leslie's knack for interior set design and flower arranging.

I was meeting Martha at a new phase in her life. The thirty-five-year-old former model-turned-stockbroker had left Manhattan a few years earlier with her husband of sixteen years, Andy, and Alexis to enjoy the small-town values and pastoral greenery that Westport had to offer.

I met Andy a few weeks later; it was another rustic Martha Stewart moment. I was sitting in Martha's kitchen having a morning coffee. Andy walked in wearing a buffalo plaid shirt and rimless glasses. In each hand he carried a large cage that held several of Martha's prize hens.

"Martha, where do you want these?" he asked his wife with a hopeful smile.

"Over there," she said without glancing up.

I could see right away that these two had different personalities and temperaments but seemed to work well as a couple. She was in charge and had a million things to do, and he was there to support her.

Since I lived just a few blocks away and because Leslie was fast becoming close friends with Martha, I became a frequent visitor to the Stewart household over the next few years. Martha and I were simpatico from the start in a very important way: we both love the simple things in life, which we truly believe can be big and exciting.

Despite all rustic appearances, I was soon to learn that the Stewarts were not your typical conventional suburban family—they were much more than that.

My first tipoff was the swimming pool in the backyard. To the shock of some of her conservative neighbors, Martha had painted her entire pool black. The idea came to her in a flash, she explained to me; she had a vision of her pool as one of those shimmering, depthless rectangles you see in the front of a museum. She had bought buckets of black paint and brushes and transformed the pool by herself. Knowing Martha, she most likely did it to keep the water warmer. There would be no pool heater for this not-so-recently ordained Connecticut Yankee.

"Come over and swim anytime you want," she said when she saw me admiring her black lagoon. I took her up on the invitation, and during my mornings off working as a clothing designer on Seventh Avenue, I'd hop on my bike and ride over to Martha's to take a cool dip.

When I arrived, I usually found Martha working in the garden. She would be sitting on the ground, legs folded to one side, her hands gloved, weeding around one of the various perennials that surrounded the early-nineteenth-century farmhouse on Turkey Hill Road that she had lovingly renovated and restored.

Martha's hands were never idle, I discovered; there was just too much to be done. As soon as she noticed that your hands were conspicuously at your sides with nothing to do, she found something to keep you busy.

After my dip in the pool, I'd hear her voice filter through

the zigzagging rows of perennials, "Lloyd, do you think you could . . . ?" I would happily pick up a trowel to help her dig and plant whatever she had in mind.

It's hard to describe how it happened, but Martha had a way of making you want to help and be involved. It was as if whatever she was doing—even if it was pulling weeds from the mud on hands and knees—was the most interesting thing to do at the moment.

I must admit that I liked to help her because I knew there was often a tasty reward in it for me at the end of my labors. As I pulled out weed after weed, Martha would disappear into the house; fifteen minutes later she'd poke her head out of the kitchen window and call, "Lloyd, come on in and have some lunch!"

Hanging out with Martha usually meant working or eating, usually both. Inside her kitchen, which was adorned with hanging copper pots and beautifully colored chicken eggs laid by her dozens of hens, we'd indulge in our mutual passion: food. Leslie was often there with me, and we would sample whatever Martha had in the fridge or cooking on the stove, analyzing the ingredients, aromas, textures, and tastes. We'd stand around the counter devouring chive biscuits with herb butter, smoked chicken, minimuffins, and orange wedding cake.

One afternoon, as I rounded the corner in front of her house on my bike, Martha saw me from the window and ran out to the yard, waving, with her oven mitts still on her hands. "I just pulled a quiche from the oven!" she said.

For probably the fifth time that week, I stood in her kitchen and hovered over her stove, sniffing appreciatively.

"Stand back, it's hot," she warned, and then told me the day's special. "It has spinach and onions and some nice Gruyère cheese."

I noticed another work in progress on the counter. "What's this one going to have in it?" I asked.

"You help me decide. Have a taste." She handed me a fork and asked what was missing.

Together, we tasted and added a little of this and a sprinkle of that. That's what cooking with her was like back then—relaxed and experimental.

Because Martha raised chickens and other fowl, eggs were fresh and plentiful in her home; I ate a *lot* of quiche. I can't remember how many birds she owned at the time, maybe two dozen or more, but every day she'd go to the henhouse and gather eggs in a wire basket. Sometimes Leslie would get them, sometimes Alexis would. Often I was the one with the basket, alone in the warmth of the coop, surrounded by clucking sounds as the hens moved to get out of the way of my interfering hands. When someone new moved in on her street, Martha often showed up at their doorstep with a basket of her eggs or vegetables from her garden as a welcome-to-the-neighborhood gift.

If I dropped by at Martha's at the start of a busy workday, after she became a caterer, it was like standing in the eye of a hurricane. There would be a dozen people in the kitchen taking over every inch of counter space, bumping into one another, flour airborne everywhere. Martha would be wearing her uniform of choice—a soft denim work shirt, white chinos, and a pair of white Keds. She'd bark out orders left and right as she stirred something on the stove or seized something from the oven.

Andy would drift in and out of the room running errands, and a yawning Lexi would come down in her pajamas, grab a bowl of cereal, and try to no avail to get her mother's attention; in moments like this, attention was impossible.

The catering team was always working against the clock and under Martha's perfectionist vision. *This needs more salt and did you remember to take the biscuits out of the oven and someone get some cilantro from the garden right away before the oil and vinegar separates.* You could cut the tension in the kitchen with a Wusthof paring knife. It was a controlled sort of chaos, though, where there was always work to be done: food to be cooked, ribbons tied, photographs shot, gardens tended, pies baked, trees pruned, flowers arranged, photographs reshot, wood measured, then cut and nailed, and chickens fed.

Once in a while Martha and her catering team broke for a bit of silliness. I remember walking into the kitchen one day when one of the women turned on a Rod Stewart cassette tape; there was Martha in the middle of the kitchen, swaying to the music and belting out the lyrics with as much huskiness as she could muster as the rest of the women danced around: *If you think I'm seeeeexxxxy and you like my booooooodddddy, come on sugarrrr let me knooooowwwwww!*

But that was very rare. Most of the time, Martha would be so engrossed in her quadruple-tasking that almost every afternoon she would suddenly look up at the clock and gasp, "Oh my God, we have to pick up Lexi from school!"

Since Martha was usually arms deep in either food or dirt, she'd toss the car keys to whomever had a free hand—the stylist, the photographer, the woman rinsing the veggies, *me*—and we'd hightail it out of there and go get Lexi. It became part of the frantic, comic routine in that kitchen. Lexi, by the way, usually wasn't disappointed when it wasn't Mom who showed up in front of her school in her Chevy Suburban.

"Oh, it's *you*. Good," she'd say, getting into my red pickup and shutting the door. "Good. I mean, like, can you imagine what it's like when your mother picks you up at school covered in flour from head to toe? And wearing *clogs!*"

From early morning to late in the evening against the backdrop of the frenzied kitchen, family dramas played out in daily vignettes. Martha played the part of the matriarch against the adolescent attitude of teenage Lexi, and both were balanced by Andy's relaxed presence. The rest of us were happily bit players in the drama.

A big help to her mother, Lexi loved washing the car, working in the garden, and raking the henhouse. She excelled at repetitious tasks in the kitchen — hand her a paring knife and behold her talent. But I remember one morning when Lexi walked into the kitchen, half asleep and on her way to find some breakfast in the midst of the usual hubbub.

"Lexi, go out and clean up the henhouse," Martha ordered briskly, barely looking up.

"I'm not going into that cage. *You* go do it, Mother!"

"Now, Lexi, " Andy said soothingly, "don't talk to your mother that way—"

"Lexi, my hands are full," Martha continued. "If that henhouse remains in the state it's in, those hens won't be happy and won't lay as many eggs."

With a pout and a roll of her eyes, Lexi was out the door,

muttering, "I'll do it. It's not that I don't *like* to do it, you know, but when you *tell* me to do it, it takes away all the fun."

Because I was not in the family and not working under Martha's rule, I had a unique vantage point: I was close enough to watch the circus and be utterly amazed at the juggler but one step removed from being the one balancing on the tightrope.

At the end of the day after the work was done, the chaos died down. If I dropped by the house in the evening when Martha and Leslie were finishing up the last of many food-related photo shoots of the day, we'd sit at the kitchen table—Martha, Leslie, Andy, Lexi, and I—making small talk and having a glass of wine or iced tea. We'd jabber about anything that wasn't too serious—flowers, current events, antiques—all the while eating, drinking, and laughing. Martha would put out a dish of assorted cheeses, some leftovers from the shoot, and a "true" garden salad, as she called it. To make this salad she'd go out back and pull some herbs and vegetables fresh from her garden, rinse them off, chop them, and toss them together with the best extra-virgin olive oil and some fresh lemon juice.

These were the early days of Martha Stewart. Yes, she was driven and focused and busy even then, but she still found time to relax with friends. Not that she sat still for long, mind you. She'd take a sip of iced tea and a minute into the conversation would jump up and rearrange the flowers on the table or reorganize the cupboard.

On New Year's Eve 1979, Martha, Andy, Leslie, and I rang in the new decade in the kitchen at Turkey Hill. Martha put out a simple but mouthwatering spread of the best caviar, chopped onions, and crumbled fresh hard-boiled eggs on toast, and we washed it down with cold vodka poured from a glass bottle encased in a block of ice. Leslie has a great sense of humor and kept us all laughing throughout the evening, and we all made tipsy New Year's resolutions.

Martha wasn't much of a drinker and rarely kept up with the rest of us. I think she didn't like to lose control in any way. She has trouble sleeping through the night for the same reason. But I'm pretty sure we all went to sleep that last night of the seventies a little woozy and feeling good.

The postdisco eighties brought in a decade of extravagant, sometimes decadent parties, and Martha became the go-to woman, organizing glittering events for her clients at the Cooper-Hewitt and Whitney museums. Leslie usually styled for Martha at these parties, so we were often invited to attend. My favorite part was never the parties; it was the afterparties.

No matter the occasion or time, if we were in Manhattan we always stopped over at the original Papaya King on the Upper East Side for hot dogs and their coconut champagne concoction (Martha's favorite—a combination of coconut and orange juice) or the papaya drink. It was "the food of the gods," they advertised in hot pink and canary yellow neon signs outside the eatery. It didn't matter if Martha had just presented the finest foods and wines available to humanity a few hours earlier and it didn't matter if she had eaten a full portion of that elegant food; the truth is, Martha would choose a plain hot dog with mustard and sauerkraut over the finest filet mignon any day.

Our stops at the King on the way home became like a religious ritual for us. We'd race up Third Avenue, trying to synchronize the car with all green lights so we wouldn't catch any reds. We'd double park on Third Avenue and let the other cars honk while two of us memorized the orders and fetched the goods. Then the whole gang of us would sit, jammed into the car, and scarf it all down, basking in the neon lights and keeping an eye out for cops who would tell us to move on. We'd all be slaphappy and tired and goofy, and it was great. (By the way, anybody who really knows Martha knows she *still* makes the Papaya King stop whenever she can.)

Another of our favorite pastimes was to rummage through antiques stores and flea markets. Beverly Bronfeld's store was on Boston Post Road, a street between Turkey Hill and my house on Maple. It was just way too convenient for us not to stop in whenever we wanted, so we did.

Martha and Leslie liked collecting antique linens; I collected McCoy pottery and vintage jigsaw puzzles. Beverly would call us on her old-fashioned dial phone to tell us about something new that came in that she thought we'd like, and we'd be there in a flash.

Soon, Martha and I got to know each other's tastes so well that if we were in the store alone and saw something the other would want, we'd just buy it. She once found a pile of Melmac dishes and bought them for mc as sort of a joke. I loved those dishes because my mother had a set when I was a kid and Martha used to tease me about that. One day, she found them in Beverly's store and gave them to me, informing me that every mother of that era had a set of Melmac dishes because they were the only ones you could drop and not break. "Perfect for the modern-day housewife!" she said, handing them over with a grin.

Our flea market and estate sale sojourns started just after sunrise in—where else?—Martha's kitchen. Between bites of hot scones and muffins, we sat at her pine table and inspected the classified section of the *Westport News*, reading aloud the day's possibilities. A lot of people don't know this, but Martha is a bit of a ham. She'd take the morning paper in her hand, clear her throat loudly, and take on a distinguished John Gielgud–meets–Anthony Hopkins voice to recite the sales of the day: "Ahem . . . estate sale . . . thankyouverymuch . . . we have the grandddddest, most authentiiiiic family heeeeeeeeiiirlooooms . . ."

With a map spread out on the table, we plotted our route of attack. Choosing one destination over another could have far-reaching consequences, and deciphering the ad copy was more an art than a science. We mostly relied on gut feelings to lead us to our riches. Estate sales always caught our attention. Martha loved going to a house and rummaging through everything, looking for hidden treasures.

One of our favorite places was a Quonset hut known as the Do-Drop-In. This was really a prefab structure, the kind used to house military personnel or as hangars at small airports, with a semicircular roof curving down to form walls.

Dave Cohen, the owner, was a stocky fellow with an anchor tattoo on his bicep. He had truckloads of junk stacked up in dusty, unorganized piles. Martha and I were like raccoons scavenging through trash cans. Martha wasn't afraid of getting good and dirty as she searched for stuff; to her, it wasn't any different from getting muddy in her garden or in the henhouse. One could always wash and get cleaned up, and after being at Dave's, we had to do just that.

Dave's hut was so big and the piles so high, we'd lose sight of each other in the mazes of junk. If there was a group of us going—often Leslie or Martha's sister Laura would join us—we were like playful commandos covering each other against outsiders who came looking for the plunder. If Martha found something that someone in the search party would like, she'd hide it under her coat and carry it until she found us. If we gave it the thumbs down, she would always return it. Inside those piles of junk we always found *something* worth keeping that had been hiding in someone's attic or garage or bedroom for years.

"Lloyd, where are you? Leslie, get over here," Martha would half-whisper, half-yell through the piles. We'd come running or she'd come running and we'd hide behind a mountain of junk and whisper about what we'd just found—assessing it privately so Dave wouldn't see how excited we were.

"Look at this tablecloth," Martha would say. "It's got that fifties printed cherry pattern on it, and all six napkins!"

If Dave caught on that we were interested in something, he'd hike up the price. So we were always very nonchalant when we brought our collection to him to price. Martha loved a good bargain and always tried to talk Dave down a few bucks. We'd quietly pay him, and he would wrap everything in newspapers and put it in a used, wrinkled paper bag, or even better, a plastic bag from the grocery store, and send us on our way. But not before giving us hell for something. He loved giving Martha hell. Who wouldn't? She was always giving so much hell to other people that it was funny to watch her get it for a change. Dave wasn't afraid of her, and giving anyone a hard time was really his way of letting you know he liked you. If you caught hell from Dave, you knew you were on his good side.

.   .   .

Our kitchen tête-à-têtes and afternoon antiquing went on for a few years until the mid-eighties. Leslie left working with Martha to team up with a commercial director who was responsible for some of the largest advertising campaigns in America. I had gone back to my first love, music, and signed a recording contract.

After a few years of making music videos, I landed with a thud on the side of the road in Westport, Connecticut. As Martha moved from her home enterprise into television and lecturing, I moved into the fruit and vegetable business and opened a farm stand in the neighborhood.

I set up my fresh produce stand on Kings Highway on a slice of local historical farmland next to a stream and a waterfall; I was in business overnight. Within a month, the stand became a hangout for local celebrities: Paul Newman knew I was the man to come to if he wanted juicy honeydew melon; his wife, Joanne Woodward, enjoyed hanging over the picket fence to chat and pass the time; and the actress Sandy Dennis regaled me with stories about her many cats.

But it was Martha who was made for this farm stand. Everything about it appealed to her—the fresh, beautiful produce, the beauty of the perfect fruit that was my standard, and the romantic quality of the old-fashioned setup. At least once a week Martha would call or send one of her assistants to come to the stand to find the perfect baskets of peaches, tomatoes, strawberries, and more. One day I picked up the phone and heard a frantic voice: *"Martha needs cherries for the president!"*

Apparently Martha was involved with a luncheon for President

25

Bill Clinton and was searching for "the most perfect cherries that ever existed" to pile high on the green Jade-Ite cake stands as centerpieces for the tables.

I'm not going to lie: It was a little early in the season for cherries, but I considered it my patriotic duty to oblige the president and, of course, Martha. I called up a good friend of mine, who tracked down the first load of cherries on a truck heading east. The centerpieces, I heard later, were a hit.

During these years, I occasionally ran into Martha down at city hall. The town of Westport put her on the bad girl list and me on the bad boy list because we were constantly breaking one of the many city ordinances with our businesses. A few meddling neighbors ratted on us.

Martha's neighbors didn't like that she was running her catering business out of her basement; trucks and cars came and went at all hours and made a lot of noise. The people who were complaining did not seem to care that Martha was a pioneering entrepreneur years ahead of her time. Running a business from home is now a necessity as well as a choice for many women. Many of the women who worked for Martha were divorced and had kids to support, and they were grateful that they could work a job with flexible hours that allowed them to cook and bake in their own homes.

My crimes involved things like building without a permit and nailing wooden signs for fresh corn or local tomatoes on the sides of trees.

Martha and I were both stubborn and we drove everyone crazy because we wouldn't stop. I think we both might hold the town record for being hauled in for slim charges. We did what we could to fight the rules we thought were just plain silly. We would run into each other at city hall for the morning zoning meetings and wait on the wooden bench in the hallway sipping hot coffee until our names were called.

"Good morning, Lloyd," she would say.

"Mornin', Martha."

"So what have you done wrong this time?"

"Someone complained about a sign I nailed to a tree. You?"

"Oh, too many trucks on the property . . ."

Many people in town liked the idea of my farm stand, so I got good press. I was "heralding back a bygone era of simpler times," said one letter printed in the local paper. Martha, on the other hand, got bad press at the time. Even though she championed the good things in life, she was branded a "bitch" who "wanted it her way" and paid no regard to what others wanted. Martha's neighbors were wary of anything that didn't fit the status quo and had nothing better to do than to pick on her for working out of her house. I think sexism had something to do with it, too.

Not only was zoning after her, but the health department was constantly sniffing around her home to catch her for violating health codes. I'm sure, though, that they never found one germ within a hundred yards of Martha's kitchen because when she wasn't cooking, she was cleaning. I once watched her scrub a kitchen sink with such force for fifteen minutes that, she said, her arm ached.

Martha never gave up. The more the city came down on her, the more she dug in her heels. And I love her for it.

.   .   .

As with all friendships, ours had an ebb and flow, and our changing lives took us in different directions. By the early nineties, Martha and Andy had gone their separate ways, and Martha's television show and magazine, both named *Martha Stewart Living*, had taken off. She was busier than ever and so was I. Leslie and I got married and were proud parents of a beautiful baby boy, Sam, so we were sleep-deprived and kept close to home. In the fall of 1994, we welcomed our daughter, Phoebe, into the world.

One day I got an unexpected phone call. It had been a year since I had seen Martha.

"Lloyd, how would you like to be on my television show?" It was Martha's wonderful and distinctive voice.

Martha was putting together a Thanksgiving special for her show and thought it would be fun to visit the farm stand and talk shop on camera, giving me a little publicity while catching up a bit with each other.

I thought it was a great idea. A week later Martha pulled up in her Chevy Suburban with a camera crew in tow, and it was lights, camera, action under my tin roof. The cameras followed Martha and me as we picked up the yams and the fennel and discussed their merits as Thanksgiving vegetables and herbs. Martha raved about my produce and asked questions she knew her audience would learn from, such as "What's the difference between a yam and a sweet potato?" Then we discussed melons—honeydew, casaba, crenshaw. We had a great time chatting away in the sunshine by the waterfall, and it was so good to see her.

When we were finished, it was like old times. Martha invited the whole family over for Thanksgiving dinner at Turkey Hill. Unfortunately, we couldn't make it since we already had plans with Leslie's family and all the relatives.

By 1996, the year Bill Clinton was running for his second term, Martha's career was really cranking and she was to host a fundraising breakfast for the Clintons at Turkey Hill. This created quite a buzz in Westport. The *Westport News* sent their Street Beat cub reporters to walk around downtown and poll people on what they thought about what Martha was doing. One of them nabbed me as I was walking out of the post office; I was happy to tell her my thoughts about Hillary Clinton and Martha: "Both women are incredible ladies. They're both controversial, polarizing, but there is no denying they both do great things."

A week later, I got a little note in the mail from Martha on her usual 3-by-4-inch cream-colored index card in her very neat handwriting:

Lloyd,

I haven't seen you in such a long time. How are Leslie and the kids? Why don't you drop by the studio sometime with the kids and say hello?

Fondly,
Martha

She made no mention of the quote in the newspaper, but I'm certain she had seen or heard about it. After more than fifteen years of knowing Martha Stewart, I knew that she had a difficult time saying thank you or I'm sorry to people even if it was what she was feeling. Instead, she would send a note or drop off a gift. I knew the note was her way of saying thanks for supporting her and let's reconnect.

Not long after, Martha invited my children, Sam and Phoebe, to be guests on her Christmas special. The kids were thrilled. They also appeared in a Thanksgiving segment in which they sat around a table with Martha and made little turkeys out of pinecones and placemats out of construction paper. They were completely enthralled by Martha. The experience even inspired young Sam to start making his own home movies with our video camera.

In 1997, I closed my farm stand after twelve years because I felt it was time to go back to my musical career. Martha and I were both going through life transitions, but we kept in touch with an occasional handwritten note.

In 2000, Martha gave notice that she would no longer be living at Turkey Hill Road in Westport. In an article in the *New York Times Magazine*, Martha sadly wrote about how the quaint, friendly, small town she had loved had grown into another Starbucks-lined, retail-dominated town where people erected stone walls and electronic gates around their homes. She lamented a time when the grocery-store clerks would happily carry your bags to your car for a fifty-cent tip and scolded the closed-mindedness of the neighbors and city officials who had made life difficult for a woman trying to strike out on her own in the business world.

It saddened me to read that since her divorce she had lost many friends who had taken sides and there were few people left to just go and have a dinner and movie with. She wrote: "I've thought long and hard about the many changes in my life that have now forced me to seek home and comfort elsewhere. And I've concluded that they're not so odd, not so radical, not so personal — but certainly they are powerful enough to make me feel that I must leave, that I must go."

But Martha wasn't giving up, she was just moving forward. Our paths — hers and mine — would soon cross again.

2

Growing Up Kostyra

She was a cooperative girl.

—MARTHA KOSTYRA, MARTHA'S MOTHER

In my quest to fully understand who Martha Stewart is, I was drawn to her hometown of Nutley, New Jersey. I took Martha's sister Laura, who had not been back there in fifteen years, as my guide. Driving through town in May 2005, Laura was amazed at how the town had changed and how it has stayed the same.

"There's the pond we used to skate on during cold winters," said Laura as we wound our way through the streets lined with elm and oak trees. "And there's the high school where we all graduated—the library is in the back. That's where Martha used to hang out. And there is our house! Number 86. Look, my father's wisteria is in full bloom! You see the big walkway up to the front door? We used to sit on the steps in the summertime eating ice cream and watermelon. And look—my mother's laundry line is still in the backyard. Glad to see it's being put to good use." Laura took a deep breath. "I can still smell all those tomato plants and see the red fruit hanging from green stems. It was quite a sight."

Laura can see the influence of their growing-up years in all her siblings, especially Martha. Laura says:

My father was never quick to compliment; he was much better at criticizing. When I was a senior in high school, I took public speaking and debate and did very well in both. My teacher asked me to speak to the parents at back-to-school night and tell them about the trips we were taking in high school—we did some fun things like going into the city to St. John the Divine and walking up in the domes. I told the parents all about the places we had visited. I was looking around at them and everybody was beaming and my mother was sitting there smiling, and I looked at my father and he was sitting there as rigid as could be with this stern look on his face and I thought, Oh my God!

Afterward everybody said what a nice speech I gave and thank you so much. In the car on the way home my father said, "Laura, when you speak in public it would be wonderful if you could lower your voice into your chest." I remember the feeling of devastation. Why couldn't he have said something nice? I'm so careful with my own kids.

So that's the way it was. Much as she tried, my mother wasn't able to make up for it. One of her favorite expressions when I was growing up was, "Well, you shouldn't feel that way."

Every Sunday morning in Nutley the Kostyra family had a ritual. First, they would pile into the family car and go to the Polish

Catholic church around the corner, Our Lady of Mount Carmel, and pray. The kids dressed in their finest clothes—shirt and tie for the boys, dresses for the girls. There were six kids and each was separated by three years from the next. The oldest was Eric, then came Martha, Frank, Kathy, and George. Laura was the youngest.

"It was imperative that we not look like commoners," George told me. "In the winter when people would come to church in their ski coats, it was a sacrilege."

The family was religious enough that the priest from Mount Carmel, Father Czechowski, would come to the Kostyras' house every Easter to bless the food. At Christmas the family would receive communion and attend midnight mass and the Mass of the Resurrection.

"I imagine it all depends more or less on your parish, but I tried to keep up the traditions," says Martha's mother, "Big Martha" Kostyra, who is now in her nineties and still attends mass every Sunday.

In the summer of 1950, the small parish spent $4,300 to install ten new stained-glass windows depicting scenes from the Gospels. As the choir sang behind her, young Martha already had an eye for design, and she was transfixed by the bold colors and the architecture of the glass.

When church was over, the children would pile into the car again and the family would drive to the Polish bakery down the street. "My mother used to let us have a cup of hot milk. She'd pour a little coffee in and we'd dunk pieces of crumb cake," Laura remembers.

Then they'd pile into the car yet again and head home, where the kids would change out of their perfectly pressed pinafores and suits and get out the rags and buckets of sudsy water.

Waiting for them on the open carport was Dad's other car, the company car—a majestic and intimidating 1950 steel-gray Chevy Bel Air. Ed Kostyra was a salesman for the pharmaceutical company Pfizer, and every two years his company would give Ed a new car. He liked to keep it looking sharp. Among the chores assigned to the kids each week, washing Dad's car was perhaps the toughest. He held high standards and was not an easy critic with any task you did, even if you were just a kid.

Martha and her brothers and sisters would scrub and rinse and shine the outside of the car until they could see their reflections when they peered at their faces on the trunk. While Mom was in the kitchen making cabbage-filled pierogis for lunch, the children would carefully wash down the car's interior, wiping away the sticky fingerprints from the dashboard and windows.

It seemed to take them hours. When they were done, Ed would come around from the back garden to inspect their work. The kids would stand, holding their breaths, with their dirty rags at their sides.

"You missed a spot," Ed would inevitably say, pointing to a lone smudge on the windshield. "Get out the rag."

So the kids would go at it again as he watched and pointed out the water lines illuminated by the noonday sun. There was nothing like perfection. George told me:

It was inbred in us. Both my parents were into clean. My father was brutal about it. My father wanted us to be better than anyone in the neighborhood. We had to have the nicest yard, the nicest house, the nicest garden. The lawn had to be mowed in a certain way in a special pattern like

Wimbledon, up and down, up and down. The gardens had to be tilled every spring in a special way, and the edging and weeding had to be done, and it was expected that we would all learn how to do it.

In our house growing up, if there was anything on the floor—if you walked on the floor and you heard any grit—you'd grab the broom and sweep. That came from my mother. My mother would hear the crunching and she would go in the other room, grab the broom, and push it all aside. It would be all in one corner till the end of the day and then it would get swept up.

I have the clean trait in me even today. So does Martha. She's a clean freak. She likes things very, very spotless.

Laura remembers their parents encouraging all of them to be handy around the house. "My parents never prevented us from being around kitchen utilities. Carpentry tools were playthings. I actually built a bed from scratch for my Barbie doll using wood, a saw, a hammer, and nails found in our toolshed. I had a Barbie, but we didn't have the money for all that came with it. All of us knew how to use our dad's tools."

If the kids showed up at the breakfast table wearing a shirt or pair of pants with a missing button, an uneven hem, or an unraveling bit of thread, Mrs. Kostyra would send them back to their rooms to change and would make a mental note to mend the unsuitable garment that night after the kids were asleep.

"I was a perfectionist myself," Mrs. Kostyra admits. "I would iron everything to perfection. I remember one time Martha came home after she'd been visiting a friend and her mother had asked her, 'Who does your shirts? They're ironed perfectly!'"

Martha shared a bedroom with her younger sister Kathy in their three-bedroom home on Elm Place. The two slept on a double bed and divvied up one closet, one chair, and one chest of drawers between them. "Martha had the habit of grabbing the hem of her nightgown and dusting the top of her dresser with it," recalls Mrs. Kostyra with a laugh. "She tried to teach this to one of her girlfriends but when the girl tried it at home, her mother yelled at her!"

The house was decorated simply. "My mother was not a sophisticated decorator," says Laura. "The furniture was arranged all on the perimeter. Although the furniture changed over the years, for better or worse, there was always a sofa and about three upholstered chairs. We had a broken-down upright player piano for a while, which was replaced with a small grand. My mother sewed heavy drapes, which were taken down in the springtime, making the room barren all summer long, especially since the walls and ceiling were painted white. Martha got her decorating skills elsewhere!"

"My parents taught us independence," says George. "If you wanted to paint your room you could. Any color you wanted — to a point. And we were taught the correct way to paint the room. First you've got to fix the cracks in the plaster — gouge it out, put the spackle in, and fill it in."

Once the color was picked, the painting had to be done "the right way." Mr. Kostyra instructed the kids on how to hold the brush and how to paint the corners exactly one-quarter inch out. That was his way and that was the right way and that's the way it had to be done, he'd say. And if you messed it up you'd have to go back and fix it. If you got paint on the glass, forget it! You were supposed to trim that window with masking tape.

"If you wanted to go and play, you had to finish the project first, so we learned how to do it the right way," says George. "If you didn't do it right, it would be hanging over your head. The old man would say, 'You didn't do it the right way.' I got very fast at everything I did. It was instilled in me, in all of us. It always had to be perfect."

George says, "We were brought up in an environment where you didn't curse, you didn't kiss, and you washed your hands a lot. When we were growing up there was a lot of finger-pointing. It was always, 'Who did this?' The finger would be there and I would say, 'Not me!' It would just be down the pecking order. We called this 'Ed-itis.' How do you get rid of that? We grew up in it and it's prevalent in our family. Martha's got it—we all have it to some extent. To turn it around, to learn the in-between, is very difficult, and to exercise it is even harder. So it's either smiling or ripping the heck out of you."

The family ate dinner together every night. "Everyone talked a lot," remembers Martha's mother. "I would cook enough dinner on Sunday to have leftovers on Monday. That's why my son Eric doesn't like leftovers."

Mrs. Kostyra cooked hearty and savory dishes like sauerbraten, tongue, and galumpkies (stuffed cabbage), and she encouraged Martha and her sisters to learn to cook. "Martha was constantly baking various kinds of bread, experimenting with different ingredients, always asking the family to sample this or that," she says.

Martha also showed a creative flair. Once she plucked fig leaves from their tree, arranged them against a white cardboard background, and entered her design in a contest at school. She came home with a first-place blue ribbon.

Seeing her knack for nature and art, her father, an avid nature lover with his own artistic streak, devoted time to teaching Martha and her brothers and sisters how to arrange flowers and how to appreciate the vivid and varied colors and shapes growing in their backyard.

They grew roses behind the house on part of a two-level garden. On the top level, beside the roses, Ed planted vegetables: tomatoes, zucchini, beans, onions, and whatever else caught his fancy when it was the right time to plant. On the lower level were trees: fig and apple, from which Martha's mom would make preserves and jam after stewing the fruit in a big copper pot on the stove all day, with the kids stealing tastes of the sweet concoctions using the stirring spoon. Mr. Kostyra protected the fig trees in the winter by bending their supple branches over and burying the tree in the mulch.

One of Martha's favorite escapes was to sit in the tall, sturdy apple trees. She'd climb up and sit for long periods of time, observing the garden beneath her.

Ed was proud of his garden. In the warm weather, when he got home from work each day, he'd first stop in the garden to check for any new weeds that might have sprouted and to measure if the vegetables had grown.

"Oh, he was always in competition with the neighbor next door to see who could grow the longest string beans and the biggest tomatoes," says Martha Senior. "He planted something like ninety tomato plants every year. Like we needed them!" Whatever they didn't eat they'd jar or give away to the neighbors.

Ed taught his kids a respect for the earth and basic gardening techniques so that when he was away for a few days on business trips, it was the kids' job to look after the garden.

The Kostyra parents instilled in the kids a healthy competition, says George. When they became old enough to sew, each of the girls would lay out their dress patterns in different rooms of the house and crank up the sewing machine. They'd get out the scissors and pins and do their handiwork in private. "My mother would run between all of them helping them do the buttons," says George.

Then there was the final unveiling of the frocks and the friendly couture contest. The reward was that everybody had a new dress and they'd go to church and wear it. "This is what Martha has instilled in her business, a sort of friendly competition. It came from our family," George says.

Mrs. Kostyra remembers her kids' childhood as one full of good clean fun, family togetherness, and homespun adventures. "Believe me," she says, "today the children all have their differences, but in those days they all cooperated and worked together."

Games were big in the house. Sometimes the games lasted hours. The Scrabble board was always about. Martha's dad was so into Scrabble competition that "if Eddie didn't have anyone to play with, he played against himself," says Mrs. Kostyra. When Martha's aunt and grandmother came to visit, Martha's father would get out the cards and they would all play pinochle.

Martha's Uncle Gene also lived with the family, and Gene and Ed would spend hours on the front porch talking sports or politics, "trying to get the better of each other," says Martha's mother.

Despite the competition and hard work, Martha's mother says the family got along well. She bristles at the books that depict her husband, who passed away in 1979, badly. Ed Kostyra certainly was tough. He loved his kids the way a commander loves his troops and demanded a lot from them. He may have had a hard time expressing his love for them, but he did feel it, Mrs. Kostyra says.

"These people didn't know my husband," she asserts, shaking her head. "He was a good man. I was married to him for forty-two years and I never saw my husband drunk. One writer accuses him of being a drunk, of being a bully. Well, he was a bully like Martha. They are both just strong-willed. My husband was first of all very bright and well read. He was eloquent. Maybe he didn't have patience with certain things, but he was not unreasonable. He was musical—he played violin by ear."

The family spent summer evenings sitting on the front porch, reading books or listening to Ed play his violin.

"He only had one tune!" says George. "I don't know what it was but it was awful. And he drove everybody crazy. Every time he picked it up he played the same song. He had no repertoire at all. Same thing with the piano—he played the same thing over and over again."

Outside the Kostyra home, the sidewalks were consistently marked up with yellow and pink chalk for hopscotch. Martha and her friends jumped rope and rode bikes up and down the street, while under shade trees in the front lawn the boys played games of marbles. "Martha had lots of girlfriends, many of whom she has kept in touch with through the years," says Mrs. Kostyra.

"As a child, Martha didn't cause too many waves or anything," her mother remembers. "She was a cooperative girl. I had no problem with Martha, even though patience has never been one of Martha's virtues. She may not have patience, but she has other qualities."

In the winter, the kids would go sledding on side streets and skate on the pond in Kingsland Park. In the spring, one of Martha's favorite family outings was the annual Cherry Blossom Festival in Branch Brook Park, next door to Nutley. All the families in the neighborhood went with their kids and took pictures. While the other kids horsed around in the playgrounds and played horseshoes, Martha furthered her education in nature and spent the afternoons comparing the dozens of varied cherry trees.

In the summer the Kostyra family often visited good friends who had a bungalow in Babylon, New York, on Long Island. They would pack picnic lunches and go clamming on the seashore. "We'd stand in the shallow water and dig down with our toes in the sand looking for clams," says Martha Senior. "The kids just loved it! They all loved the seashore."

All the Kostyra kids grew up on Rutt's hot dogs. Rutt's Hut is a hot dog stand in Clifton, New Jersey, but it is more than that—they sell beer, famous chili, cheese fries, and onion rings. When Martha was a child, it was a hangout. It wasn't unusual for many families to plan an outing over at Rutt's. From the outside, the building looks somewhat like a log cabin. Inside it has big beams and door frames of dark wood that look as if they had been crudely shaped with a hand tool.

Martha's mother told me, "One time we took my mother-in-law, who lived down the street, to Rutt's for a hot dog and a bowl of chili. We were sitting in the car and Ed took the bowls and walked them back in to the restaurant, and I started the car. I got halfway down the road when his mother said, 'You forgot Eddie! You left Eddie behind!' I said, 'Oh my God, I forgot all about him.' It was so funny. Here he was trotting along the road behind us."

As a teenager, Martha never seemed to go through a rebellious or awkward phase. She was beautiful, but that wasn't really something the family focused on at all. Hard work was valued in the household, not good looks. Mrs. Kostyra recalls:

Martha never rebelled. She was too busy to think about rebelling. She was very studious. She spent a lot of time at the library, so much so that I think they were going to name a room after her. She read a lot, did her homework, was on the committees, worked on the prom—she was an all-around student who tried to excel. She was always on the honor roll and we never needed to encourage her to study. Eric and Martha—I didn't have to pay too much attention to them because they just took care of themselves. They knew what to do. They were self-motivated. And if she wasn't concentrating on school, she was busy making money babysitting.

Martha was so busy with school that she didn't have too many dates. I don't think she intimidated boys—we had a football breakfast at the house once, and there was always mention of this boy or that boy—but I think maybe she put romance on the back burner.

Whether Martha took much note of the boys or not, they took notice of her. She was pretty, but she didn't fuss over her looks. She wasn't the type to put curlers in her hair or anything, says her mother, but she had an eye for fashion. After she had finished reading the Sunday *Times*, Martha would flip through the pages of *Glamour* magazine.

"She liked to look nice in a dress. In those days you wore dresses," says her mother. "Martha went to a high school ball with a date and he pushed her to enter the prom competition. She was going to Nutley while he was attending Xavier in Manhattan, and she became Queen of the Ball at Xavier High School. We made her a pretty blue taffeta dress. I wish you could have seen her."

In her senior year Martha worked on the yearbook committee, on the book that bore her now notorious quote "I do what I please, and I do it with ease." Martha participated in extracurricular activities—handball, basketball, the drama club, and swimming—"but not with any great degree of seriousness," says her mother.

On Saturdays, Martha worked part-time as a salesgirl at the Janet Shop, a ladies' clothing store in Nutley, and in Manhattan at a Polish import store.

Even then, Martha's flair for sprucing up a dull room was evident when she took charge of decorating the gym for the school prom. She wasn't going out with anybody, says her mother, but Martha went with a local boy as her date anyway, and she basked in her transformation of the sweaty gym into a wonderland of balloons, crepe paper, and painted signs.

In her last year of high school, Martha also began to do a bit of modeling for local stores like Bonwit Teller. Mrs. Kostyra remembers:

> There was a girl across the street who was a model, and Martha and Dad and I thought that Martha had possibilities to pursue a modeling career to get money for college. I don't know how she got the address of this agency, but she found out soon enough that she had to go directly to an agency and not to any old modeling or photography studio that may advertise, because they're out just to make money.
>
> So she went to an agency in New York. She was sent to have her picture taken and she was sent on go-sees, and that's how she got into modeling. She did lots of jobs. I have a whole portfolio of pictures of her as a model.
>
> She landed a spot on the Groucho Marx show. She was supposed to be smoking, but she never smoked; she just faked it. It might have been Tareyton cigarettes. Every time they showed the ad, Martha made money. So she did okay with that.

When Martha did modeling jobs during the summers while living at home, her mother always waited up for her. One night she waited until well past midnight and began to worry. When Martha finally showed up at home, she explained that she'd been so tired that she fell asleep on the bus. The driver went to the end of his route, turned around to head back to Manhattan, and dropped Martha off on the corner near home.

When the time came for college, Martha had been such a good student that New York University offered her a full scholarship.

Mrs. Kostyra remembers meeting with the Nutley High School principal: "Martha had been accepted to Barnard, and her principal advised us that Barnard would be the better school for her." Scholarship or no scholarship, that was the school Martha would attend. "Well, she had to work," her mother said in her matter-of-fact tone.

Accepting employment from two sisters who lived on Fifth Avenue, Martha was given room and board in exchange for doing household chores and errands. They also asked her to do some cooking. "I think they each became a little too demanding," says Martha's mother.

Even though that arrangement ended after only one year, it was in that apartment on Fifth Avenue that Martha became acquainted with Julia Child's *Mastering the Art of French Cooking*, a book that changed her life. She pored over the recipes and learned her first lessons in French haute cuisine — the right cuts of meat for braising, the secret of the herb bouquet, the value of sautéing the garnish of onions and mushrooms separately.

Martha moved back home for the rest of the year, commuting from Nutley to school on the bus every day. Along with her studies, she continued her modeling and worked part-time at Bergdorf Goodman and Henri Bendel.

For her second year at Barnard, Martha moved into a dormitory. Her flair for fashion led her to be chosen as one of the best-dressed girls in college by *Glamour* magazine, but not even the media attention could sway Martha from her focus on her studies.

Nothing else could capture her attention, either — until she met Andy Stewart.

"Martha met Andy through his sister, Diane, who was in one of Martha's classes. It was love at first sight," says Martha's mother. "He was probably her first and only serious love interest up to that point in her life."

Martha was nineteen and Andy, who was studying at Yale, wasn't much older.

"Maybe she was too young; I don't know," says her mother. "But Martha always seemed so mature, and you hesitated to give her any advice because she thought she knew it all. She fell like a ton of bricks. He had a lot of exposure; he was worldly, his father was a stockbroker, and his mother taught Martha a lot about antiques. Everybody loved him. He was someone who could fit right in. I remember one weekend during the early courtship when I was making yeast dough for a babka cake, and he just washed his hands and jumped right in and mixed it. He liked to fit in and please. You had the feeling that he related to you, and he did. No airs."

Martha and Andy connected so well partly because they were both smart and disciplined. Says Martha Senior: "Andy was attracted to her intelligence and the fact that she wasn't afraid of hard work, for one thing. And Martha liked it that Andy was romantic. I don't know if he had a girlfriend before her or not. We didn't have any objection even though Andy was Jewish. His mother was a Christian Scientist and his father was Jewish but not observant. They were very nice people and they accepted us too even though we were different. They also accepted Martha and regarded her highly. Too bad it didn't work out. Everything was there to make it work."

George remembers:

When Martha brought Andy home to meet the family in New Jersey, it was a rather interesting situation. Andy wore denim coveralls. He was a preppie, but he liked to work the fields, use his hands, do things, mow lawns. It was a great fit, because that's the way we were. We were the same as everybody else on the street—working families—but somehow my father thought we had an aristocratic background, even though our great-grandparents were probably farmers in Poland.

Martha was doing some sort of project at Barnard and she and my father went to the library together and did a family tree all the way back to the fourteenth century. They came back home with a picture of a coat of arms traced back to the Isle of Kos off the Greek coast. They somehow devised a pattern of immigration into the heartland of Europe, into Poland. My father said our ancestors were horse people who rode for the king. They created this mythology for our family background, and I think Martha really believed it.

I remember Andy asking my father for my sister's hand in marriage. We were all huddled in the kitchen with our ears to the door wondering what was going on. And then that whole thing with the diamond ring—it's been reported that the first one wasn't large enough and he had to go back to Harry Winston and get a larger one. But really all Martha wanted was a setting more befitting her hand.

Despite her dad's concerns, "Andy fit right in, he was really so nice," says Martha's mother. "We would have the eggs blessed at

Easter time and we'd wish each other good luck and good health and he was right there like the member of the family that he was. Martha was rather young compared to today's brides, but I always had the feeling that she knew what she was doing."

"They seemed very much in love," says Laura. "He was a wonderful big teddy bear kind of guy, and he paid a lot of attention to me," she says.

By her last year at Barnard, Martha knew two things. First, that she was soon to have a new name, Martha Stewart. And second, that she was destined for great things.

3

Keeping Home

It may sound corny, but my mother loves
every second of everything—she does!

—ALEXIS STEWART

Martha and Andy had a small wedding at St. Paul's Chapel, Columbia University, with only family attending. It was very unlike the current Martha wedding style—nothing formal and the ceremony was simple. The bride wore white.

"I was five years old, so I was quite young," says Laura. "My mother made us our outfits and Martha sewed her own dress. I had on a little yellow number with a yellow band for my blond hair."

After the ceremony, Andy's father pulled up in his Jaguar to pick up the newly married couple and drove them to the reception in the Barberry Room at the Berkshire Hotel.

"We weren't allowed to go to the reception," remembers George, who was ten at the time. "Laura and I kept asking, 'Why can't we go? Why can't we go? The adults told us we were just too young."

Martha graduated from Barnard and continued to model. Andy enrolled at Yale Law School. Martha and Andy moved to a little farmhouse in Guilford, Connecticut, near New Haven. To the rest of the Kostyra kids, that rundown farmhouse was paradise.

"For us, it was a big escape," says Laura, "getting out of Nutley, going to be with Martha and Andy. I remember a few times when my mother wouldn't let me go for some reason or other and I'd be just devastated. I remember crying and carrying on and saying, 'How unfair!'"

After Andy graduated from law school, the couple rented a rambling apartment on Riverside Drive and 101st Street in Manhattan—"one of those beautiful old apartments with multirooms, big rooms. You wandered through hallways," says Laura.

Martha and Andy made frequent trips to Nutley to visit with Martha's family.

"Martha helped support the family when my father was out of work," George recalls. "She was very caring—both of them were—and they sort of adopted my sister and me."

Martha and Andy, now sophisticated adults living in the big city, considered it their duty to show the younger Kostyra kids life outside the suburbs. Martha and Andy started looking for property to buy in upstate New York and Massachusetts, and they took Laura and George along for road trips, stopping at antiques stores and museums along the way.

"They thought we needed to be out in the world experiencing things instead of being in Nutley living a mundane lifestyle, so they would ask Laura and me to come and be with them on weekends," says George, "which I thought was very generous. Andy had this little teeny round Mercedes 200, 1957, I think, and we drove that around till it died. I remember going up to

Cape Cod, camping out on the dunes, and looking at farm properties in Woodstock, New York. Martha and Andy loved to see auctions and farm properties, historical societies, gardens — every weekend was packed full of all these things to do. We would stay at motels, friends' houses, wherever, because there was no money. We'd eat basic diner food."

"Antiquing was a huge activity," says Laura. "Andy's mother really knew her antiques. Andy grew up in a somewhat privileged home and traveled a lot. His mother, Ethel, gave Martha an education in what antiques were, so of course Martha wanted to have antiques immediately. At that time, they were affordable for two people like Martha and Andy on their budget. I remember we went up to Nyack, New York, once a month for this wonderful auction. We would walk around previewing all the great stuff; they would pick out a piece of furniture and it would appear in their home a short time later. Martha started bidding early in her life at auctions. Now of course you see her at Sotheby's with a lot more money to spend."

In early 1965, Martha discovered she was pregnant. "She was so excited," says her mother. "She and Andy were both thrilled." As Martha's pregnancy progressed, she stopped modeling. Alexis Gilbert Stewart was born on September 27. "I used to change her diapers and take care of her," says George. "She was like a little sister to me and I felt very responsible toward her."

Lexi was exposed to more than most kids when it came to literature, art, and culture in general. Her mother never failed to include her in activities normally reserved for older children or adults. Martha had bettered herself and was determined that her daughter wouldn't be left behind.

"My favorite time with my parents ever was when we would be on car trips and my mother would read a book out loud to me," says Lexi. The reading material ran from Aesop's fables and Grimm's fairy tales to Edgar Allan Poe's "The Raven" and from Oscar Wilde's "The Nightingale and the Rose" to John Irving's *The World According to Garp*.

Looking back, Lexi says, "The reading material might have been considered slightly inappropriate, but I was mature, or at least they thought I was. That's what all our trips were like. Reading made the trip go faster. It's why I took up reading at an early age and why I read today. I still rarely watch television. My mother loved to read and I love to read. I have always read, and now if I am in the car alone, I listen to audiobooks."

Soon after Lexi was born, Martha and Andy bought a nineteenth-century schoolhouse in Middlefield, Massachusetts, in the Berkshire foothills. The house had no running water or plumbing; Martha had to haul buckets of water from a nearby stream to the house to cook and wash with. In the five years it took to renovate the house, Martha and Andy lived the happy rural life of a couple of hippies, minus the drugs.

Most weekends, Laura and George would take the bus to Manhattan, then they'd all drive out to the farmhouse to work on it. George recalls:

Laura and I would jump on the bus to the Port Authority in Manhattan. I was twelve or thirteen, and she was three years younger. I was in charge of holding her hand and running through the subway stations. We would get off at 103rd

Street and walk two blocks south to Martha's apartment. The woman who cared for Lexi would let us in. Martha and Andy would get off work at five thirty and by six o'clock we would be packed into the car and off to Massachusetts.

We'd work all weekend. They bought a tractor and I would mow lawns. I learned how to use a chainsaw. It was fun. I remember one phrase they would always say. We'd go, "How do we move this big rock?" and they'd say, "How did the Egyptians do it?" We'd cut down a tree and use it as a lever.

We did everything by hand. There was no money even to rent a backhoe. Ten years later after I had dug a sixty-foot trench for a septic line, Andy got a backhoe in there for something and it was $150 and he said, "Oh, if I had known it was going to be so little, I would have brought it in for the trench," but meanwhile I grew some muscles.

Those days were really fun. I remember when Lexi was about three and we were sitting outside and the nasturtiums were coming up. We picked things out of this little teeny garden and brought them inside to show Lexi. I didn't know what they were; I was learning right along with Lexi. Martha held up a bright yellow flower speckled with pink. "What flower is this, Lexi?"

"*Nasturtiums!*"

Lexi remembers her early education in nature: "I've been told that at one time I knew every plant by its Latin name. I doubt I knew every plant—maybe I did; I was a kid and not paying attention to the details—but the fact that my mother took the time to teach me the proper names is astonishing. She was always teaching me something. That's my mother in a nutshell. If you can teach her something, she will listen to you. If she doesn't understand, she will ask questions. She is fascinated with acquiring knowledge. She actually does know just about every plant by its Latin name, and she sure knows the trees and shrubs. Ask her about any of them and you will get a lecture."

George describes their time in Middlefield in the late sixties and early seventies as a romantic back-to-nature experience. The family raised their first chickens at the farmhouse.

"It was all about going and finding a piece of land and living off it, learning how to get back to nature," says George. "Listening to banjos, listening to folk music, discovering Leadbelly and the Mamas and the Papas. We use to have the greatest evenings with a bunch of hospitable people. Everybody had their guitars out and was constantly singing. Martha would make pies and other things for the occasions. Sometimes she would bring a bushel of peas and we'd all shuck them. We would spend hours picking wild blueberries—you know, the little bitty ones. Then when we got back, Martha would make a pie or bread. We had so many blueberries, we had to keep thinking up new things to do with them."

One Friday night after staying in the city all week, Andy, Martha, and Lexi came up to the Middlefield house, where George had been staying, to spend the weekend. George remembers:

I got home at five o'clock and I cleaned the whole house. I vacuumed everywhere just to make it nice for when they arrived. I got a fire ready to go in the fireplace. They arrived, and Martha walked in and said, "Hi, George. We're here. How are you doing?" And then she got the vacuum out and started vacuuming.

I said, "Martha, I just finished doing that."

She looked at me and said, "You don't understand. This is what I *do*."

"But I just finished doing the whole house!"

"I have to do this! This is what I do when I get here!"

So I said, "Okay, next week I'm not doing it."

And she said, "That's fine."

That was her routine. She couldn't help herself. She had to make sure that everything was spotless.

Hanging out in Middlefield was a great way for the family to get to know Andy.

Laura says, "Growing up in my family, there was a lot of competition to be heard. If I was talking at the dinner table, more times than not I would get cut off and interrupted and the subject was changed. So I would be sort of shoved under the table. I grew up feeling that my opinion didn't really count."

As a teenager, Laura vividly remembers being at a dinner party given by friends of Martha and Andy's. She was seated next to her brother-in-law.

"I just sat at the table and I would not talk; I would just listen. People said something to me and I would say yes or no. Finally Andy asked, 'How come you never talk?' I said, 'Nobody wants to hear what I have to say. What could I say that is new?' And then he said something that was so profound. He said, 'It doesn't matter if they've heard it a hundred times, they've never heard it from *you*.' I just thought, wow. It didn't open me up right away, but it gave me something to think about. Andy made you feel wanted and comfortable."

On the way back to New York, they usually stopped to eat at a little hamburger spot on the highway or at a spaghetti place in Danbury, Connecticut.

By the time Lexi was a toddler, Martha was looking for a new career. She decided to enter the financial world. She passed the stockbroker's exam with ease and registered with the New York Stock Exchange in 1968 at the age of twenty-seven. She became highly successful.

With Martha pulling in a six-figure salary and Andy working as a high-powered corporate attorney at this point, they were sitting pretty for a while. But they also eventually grew tired of city life. By 1973, Martha had quit her job on Wall Street and bought another old farmhouse, this time in Westport, Connecticut. She dubbed it Turkey Hill.

"The house needed nothing but work," Lexi remembers. "There wasn't a door handle on the front door for years. 'There are more important things,' my mother would say. My mother has always been into locating and restoring old things. She loves the history of it all and that's what we moved into: a historical, dusty, broken-down old house. If she wasn't cooking, gardening, or catering, she was working on the house. My mother and father did most of the work and my uncle George enjoyed pitching in. Carpentry's his thing and he was a great help. Me, I liked to play and get in the way. I might have cleaned a little. I was still young and that was about all my parents could let me do."

George brought up one of his fraternity brothers from Rutgers that first summer and together they painstakingly scraped and painted the outside of the house white. George remembers:

Martha had a big vegetable garden. One day she said, "From now on we are going to live off the land! We are going to just buy the basic staples from the food store. So you go down and catch some bluefish or whatever you can get out of the water." Catching enough fish took forever. We'd often have dinner down at Berring Hill Beach and we'd cook some snapper. Or I'd bring a pail and we'd go crabbing. We ate zucchini, corn, and tomatoes—she was using all these things from the garden to make salads—and Martha had the chickens, so we ate lots of eggs. That lasted a few weeks, then the garden dried up. Everything that could be picked had been picked.

Lexi cherishes the close mother-daughter moments they had in the early years in Westport. The two could often be seen around town in their matching short-shorts and bathing suit tops, and, before big business invaded their house, it was just Lexi and Mom in the kitchen. Lexi recalls:

One of the first things my mother taught me to bake was a velvet spice bundt cake. I was in third grade. My mom never prohibited me from being in the kitchen around hot stoves and skillets. It was quite the opposite. She thought children should learn skills as early as they possibly could, and not just in the kitchen. My mother wants everyone to be self-sufficient. She thinks that makes a better world and all that intellectual stuff. Knowledge to her isn't the three Rs so much as the big S: learning *skills*, any skill, and the more skills you know, the further you will get in life.

She taught me how to whip egg whites and fold them into the batter. I learned to turn the cake precisely 180 degrees to ensure equal browning. And she always used currants in the cake, but I tired of picking them out and decided I'd make the cake my way so that I wouldn't have to deal with them ever again. The recipe came from the *Joy of Cooking*.

I just might be a better cook than my mother. My mother says so, anyway. I'm less rushed than she is. She just wants it done.

I can't imagine how many recipes my mother knows by heart. It's some outrageous number. My mother always cooked the family meals and never missed cooking on a holiday. She wouldn't think of it. Everyone knows that holidays are my mother's favorite times of the year. She learned how to cook from her mother and she taught me. How many kids do you think know how to cook nowadays? It's sad when you can't do that one very important task. The reasons are obvious why you should know how to cook. I'm glad she had a passion for food and for cooking.

Martha decorated the farmhouse with Ball jars filled with baking supplies, and with pottery and fresh flowers, and she set forth on her mission to fill the house with unique furnishings. She enlisted George's help and the two ventured off to local tag sales every Friday morning no later than seven A.M.

"George, go up to this place and get tickets and stand in line!" she'd tell him. While they waited for the doors to open, Martha could spot through the windows which pieces she wanted. When they unlocked the gates and everybody rushed in, Martha moved quicker than most.

"She would just run through," George remembers with a laugh, "and we would grab tickets off the furniture and this and that. She had the ability to see things from afar that were of consequence; it was unbelievable. Some people complained about Martha grabbing things out from under them while they were considering it, but that was what tag sales were all about! If you didn't grab what you wanted, someone else got it. Some people were just more adept at it than others and Martha was one of them."

Laura recalls:

> Martha called me one day from Texas and said, "There's a fabulous tag sale going on in Fairfield. You have to go and get numbers and I'll come later." She had heard about it from her little network. So I got there early and got my ticket and was standing in line, waiting for Martha to show up. I overheard a woman saying to somebody else, "Did you see Martha Stewart get here and grab all the tickets at such and such a time!"
>
> I said, "No, Martha didn't get here at that time."
>
> "Yes she did! I know who Martha Stewart is."
>
> "Well I'm Martha's sister and she called me from Texas this morning!" All these rumors of Martha doing this and Martha doing that. She was the bad girl of the tag sale scene."

Martha was focused on making their house into a beautiful home. "They never stopped working on that house," says George. "People would come over and they would never stop working while visitors were there. And the visitors would feel like they had to pitch in. Some were uncomfortable doing that. There was always something to do; that was part of her image and his. You couldn't sit down. It was the great American work ethic—Martha is a workaholic. It's part of my family's makeup—everybody works at something.

"She loved the Shakers and so did Andy. They designed the house around the Shaker mentality—it was either so expensive that you didn't sit in it or it was so hard and uncomfortable to sit in that you kept working."

Years later, when Andy went to George's house and sat down in the living room, "He said, 'This is *great*, I can put my feet up on stuff! I wish my house was like that.' I said, 'Andy, you can have this,' and he said, 'No . . . I can't.' They didn't want it. They'd go out and buy these fancy antiques and things that would appreciate in value. But could you sit in them? That's another question."

George, too, became enamored of Westport. A few years after Martha moved to the quaint little town, he followed.

"I didn't know anybody and I was moping around and Martha said, 'What's wrong with you? Why don't you put a smile on your face?' I was bummed out that I had moved and didn't have a job."

Martha went into autopilot big-sister mode and said, "A friend of mine over on Cross Highway needs someone to wash her windows. I want you to go over and help."

"Why would I want to go wash her windows?" George asked.

"They're having a party this weekend. Just get over there, help wash windows, and you'll have a good time."

She was right. George went over on Thursday morning and "I didn't go home until Sunday night. I met all these great people and they were so eccentric and we partied all the time. If it hadn't been for Martha, I never would have been introduced to them. Martha gave me the opportunity to meet people. She put me in situations that were new to me where I might survive or might not—situations that I might get something out of or not. But it was up to me to make that choice."

George credits Martha with teaching him most of what he knows about architecture, design, and aesthetics because she was interested in it all and exposed him to it. Her guidance led George to his current career as a house remodeler.

Soon after he moved to Westport without a job, Martha and Andy offered him the job of building their barn.

"It was just going to be a job for a couple of months, but then when I went to get the permits, I discovered it had to have a bathroom and a septic system—the list went on and on and on. It was a very creative but difficult job. I learned how to do the research and ask the questions. I took courses and with that training I got more involved in the construction business. Martha wanted me to be an architect, but I just didn't have the inclination. I like doing what I'm doing—the hands-on side."

In the late seventies, Lexi went through the joys and angst of growing pains. In school, at Greens Farms Elementary and Greens Farms Academy, she excelled in her classes. An honor student, she loved to arrive early in the morning for classes. She did her homework with zeal and she read constantly, just like her mother. Her only rebellion in the house was her yen for junk food. Lexi says:

> My friends and I would always make virgin eggnog. That was our drink. Why eggnog? Because my mother never allowed any junk food in the house, so I had to come up with my own junk food and eggnog was about as close as I could get. The house contained only ingredients. Understand? No finished products, no snack food, no fast food, no nothing.
>
> My mom loves using fresh ingredients—not only for flavor but for the health benefits too. My mother was always cooking. I learned to cook by helping her in the kitchen. When I went to friends' homes I always raided their pantry. I was a kid!

At Beverly's Collectibles, Beverly Bronfeld remembers that Martha often brought Lexi into her store. During one Christmas holiday, "I had this beautiful silver party dress. Martha loved it and wanted Lexi to have it, but as with most teenage girls, anything that a mother liked, the daughter didn't." Martha, naturally, bought it anyway. "She said to Alexis, 'You may not appreciate it now, but one day you will.'"

To this day, Lexi still does not agree that her mother was any more controlling than other mothers. But Martha has laughingly said that Lexi calls her by the pet name Mommie Dearest. Says Lexi, "We've fought about her trying to control me. Most daughters fight with their mothers about that issue. Your mother would like it her way and you want it your way. I probably try to control her as much as she tries to control me. What are you going to do? That's life. My mother cared about how my room was decorated and arranged. It wasn't an option. I had my shelves; she built me shelves so that I could have all my stuff neatly organized. I was happy with it. When I brought home a boy, she asked questions. Is that being controlling?"

Lexi dutifully helped her mother in the early stages of Martha's catering business, at the same time whining and complaining with a condescending *tsk!* — "Oh, mother . . . *tsk* . . . those weddings are the *worst!*" — only to get the same reply from Mom: "Oh, *Lexi* . . ."

"It was a period I went through," Lexi says. "Having all the people in my house got to me one summer. It was like all these people were under my feet. Using our dishes, the bathroom, having the run of the house and feeling like they owned it. Annoyed doesn't come near describing the way I felt."

At one point, her aunt Laura pulled her aside and gently scolded her: "Lexi, it's rude when you make that noise, *tsk!* — can't you refrain from that?"

Contrary to media reports that Martha never paid enough attention to her daughter, Lexi insists:

I actually wanted her *less* involved than she was! All kids want to kind of break away. My mom always wanted to know what I was up to and whom I was hanging out with. She worked from home! I saw her every day when I lived there.

I was involved with her business, too. I worked for her. I helped her with cooking and baking and even made wedding cakes with her. She involved me in her whole life. What other parent can say that? Just find me one.

I might have had an attitude problem. It's an old story that we all go through, but when it comes to my mother and me it is so blown out of proportion it makes me sick. This is human nature, this is growing up, this is normal interaction between parents and kids. If you believe what you read, then our relationship was unique. I doubt that. As close as parents are to their children, they all have good times and bad times.

When Lexi was thirteen, Martha enrolled her at the prestigious boarding school Choate Rosemary Hall in Wallingford, Connecticut, an hour's drive away. Andy himself had been educated in Switzerland and had grown up in boarding schools.

"It was the nicest gift my mother and father gave me," she says. "My mother understood the pressures she was putting on me at home. People think I was sent away so they wouldn't have to deal with me; pouty Lexi gets sent away! *Hello?* We discussed it. It was my decision in the end, and my parents wanted me to go to a good private high school. I'd come home on weekends. Sometimes I'd bring a friend, sometimes boyfriends."

Necy Fernandez, Martha's former housekeeper, started to work for Martha at about this time and observed Lexi on her visits home on weekends or vacations. "She would come to spend time with her mother and father. Lexi was very quiet. She'd stay in the house and read books and she'd help her mother. She also liked to organize things around the house. She is a hard worker like her mother. When she was home she would clean the house or wash her car."

With Lexi away at school, Martha got two chow dogs, Max and Zuzu, to keep her company.

Turkey Hill became a flurry of activity. Martha was on the verge of a new career, and people were coming and going. The garden out back where Martha and Andy had planted flowers and vegetables was always in lush, erupting bloom.

"If you look at Martha's gardens—I don't know what it is, but at any place she plants, it grows ten times better than anywhere else," says George. "I've never understood it. It's her energy or something."

4

No Limits

Something like Fauchon.

—MARTHA STEWART

*I*f you're interested in getting involved in the most exciting food concept in Fairfield County and if you are a wonderful baker or a good cook, please call this phone number . . .

It was the late seventies, and women were donning shoulder pads fit for a linebacker as they entered a fierce new battlefield: the male-dominated corporate workplace. And here was a bold, intriguing little ad in the classified section of the Westport News offering women a different kind of power—to be creative and turn a profit in their own kitchens. Connecticut housewives sat at the breakfast table on that snowy January morning in 1978, gulping their first coffee after getting the husbands and kids out the door and reading about Martha's "most exciting" little promise.

I had been Martha's neighbor for a year at this point, and I knew her well enough to foresee what she was cooking up in that extraordinary brain of hers. She had already been catering for small dinner parties, whipping up fabulous gourmet meals for twelve in her kitchen at Turkey Hill and delivering them to hostesses about town, who would then smile and tell guests they'd been slaving over a hot stove all day.

Since Martha can never stay in one place or at one level for long, it was time for her to expand this venture. With much charm, she managed to convince the owner of a quaint little clothing shop, the Common Market, to let her commandeer a corner of the store where she would sell delicious baked goods in pretty market baskets. In exchange, she would give the owner a percentage of her profits. She already had the baskets — flawed but beautiful wicker and bamboo baskets collected over years of roaming that were hanging all over the walls and ceilings at Turkey Hill. The owner liked the idea and struck a deal with Martha.

Now she needed the power to fill those baskets. Of all her creative and business talents, Martha instinctively knew that the real key to a successful business is to surround yourself with talented devotees. Martha had a knack for spotting creative people and convincing them to follow her.

"Martha has a good eye, " says Louise Felix, who worked with Martha for six years during this time. "She knows when a house has good bones, she knows when a recipe has good flavor, and she knows when a person has good skills, and that's an ability in itself."

The day the advertisement ran in the paper, Martha's phone began ringing. Within the next forty-eight hours, all the great unknown chefs of Westport were to make their pilgrimage to Martha's front door.

. . .

Audrey Doneger had never held down a job outside of her home before. She left college and got married, then had five children in six years.

"I loved raising my children and my only other constant love was cooking, but as the years went by, I felt more and more worthless. My contributions weren't valued, and I don't think I was ever complimented on anything but my food. With my kids fleeing the nest, my world was shrinking fast. When all my children were finally out of the house making their own families, the loneliness really began to set in."

She took a gamble, perhaps the first in her life, and called up Martha.

"The first thing she said to me was that she wanted to do, and she used these words, 'something like *Fauchon.*' I heard and felt the silence on the line as she waited to see if I knew what she was talking about. I knew exactly. Fauchon in Paris was the most remarkable food store I had ever seen; it sold beautifully prepared foods. There were no Zabar's, no Silver Palates at this time. If you wanted prepared food, you went to a deli or ordered Chinese takeout and that was it. Martha was way ahead of the trend in this country."

"Would you like to audition for me?" Martha asked. Audrey was taken aback and hesitated a bit before awkwardly replying, "Audition? I . . . well . . . yes!"

The food scene at the time was a health kick—lots of carrot cake and bean sprouts—but Audrey didn't do any of that tofu type of baking. You would never see a soy cookie or a mock chicken at Fauchon. Audrey's dishes were unabashedly full of eggs and heavy cream and butter and salty bacon and aged exotic cheeses and rich chocolate.

Audrey put together a dream basket full of her favorites: Coquilles St. Jacques, pâté, chocolate chip cookies made with chunks of real dark chocolate, and three other kinds of cookies that were the rage with her kids and their friends—pecan crescents; thimble cookies, the center of which she pressed with her thumb and then filled with jam or whatever else would strike her; and meringue cookies made with egg whites, nuts, and chocolate. Audrey topped off the basket with the sweet she was to become famous for, her tangy lemon bar.

"I packed it all in with a gingham cloth napkin and off I went to Martha Stewart's house with my basket of goodies. I felt like Little Red Riding Hood facing the big bad wolf, especially when I saw a very dejected woman walking out of Martha's house. I could see this woman's carrot cake sitting on Martha's table as I walked in. I was mesmerized by the fabulous kitchen I had entered. It was almost magical. I remember Martha being very dynamic but cordial, pleasant but businesslike." After all, this was a job interview.

Martha placed the basket on the kitchen table, undraped the gingham, and took out each item, lining them up on her pine table where she had a row of spoons and forks laid out, ready for the inspection. With Audrey watching nervously, Martha proceeded to take a taste of everything. She didn't say a word, but you could see a little smile when Martha tried the pâté, and a thoughtful nod when she tasted the Coquilles St. Jacques, and her eyebrows slightly lifted in surprise when she took a bite of a lemon bar.

"She loved it all," recalls Audrey with a smile. "But it was only after she tasted my cookies that she said, 'These are *perfect*. How would you like to work for me?' I was flabbergasted. I didn't think; I said, 'I'd love to.' And then Martha said, 'Okay. Then I want you to go home and make . . .'"

Audrey already had her first assignment: to produce a giant batch of the cookies Martha had declared perfect. There was no time to waste; Martha wanted to get those cookies into a basket and into the store pronto. They were just too good not to share immediately, she insisted.

Excited, Audrey rushed home and baked all night. It was the first time she had ever made so many cookies at once. She had waxed paper on every piece of furniture, on every surface—it covered her house. At three o'clock in the morning, she was still baking cookies, measuring each batch out, thinking, I really don't know what I'm doing!

By five A.M., her arms aching, she placed an emergency call to her sister-in-law, whose parents owned a housewares store and had stocked the newest item in vogue—a Cuisinart food processor. "I will meet you at the New Rochelle toll booth. Put a Cuisinart in your car; I need it." They were very expensive and Audrey couldn't really afford it, but she didn't care. She picked it up, came home, and finished up her order by eight A.M.

"The next morning I went to the Common Market with my cookies. I waited while Martha silently tasted each cookie. You don't schmooze with Martha. She's not going to have a pajama party with you. She's a different species."

A puzzled look came over Martha's face when she bit into one cookie from the Cuisinart batch, then a knowing frown.

"Oh Audrey, you are such a good cook—what happened with that cookie?"

Audrey couldn't believe it. My God, she thought, she can tell the difference between the ones I made by hand and the ones I didn't. There was no fooling her, so Audrey confessed. "Oh Martha, I got so tired because I was doing this all by hand, and I figured I could do it in the Cuisinart."

"I'll tell you what I want you to do," Martha told her, taking a wad of bills from her purse and pressing it into Audrey's palm. "Go out and buy all the butter you want, all the sugar, all the flour you need, and teach yourself to make cookies in larger batches."

Within a few weeks, Martha recruited more staff for her culinary team in much the same way. Vicky Sloat was looking through the classifieds when Martha's ad caught her eye. On Martha's snow-covered front porch, Vicky deposited a whimsical basket lined with hand-painted napkins and filled with chocolate soufflé rolls, miniature scones, star-shaped cookies, and watercolored recipe cards for the whole lot. Hired!

Sarah Gross was waiting tables and working in an organic market when she auditioned with her strawberry nut torte and chocolate chip cookies. Hired!

Vicky, Sarah, Audrey, and Martha's sister Laura were part of the core team of cooks along with Martha who began to wow the town's tastebuds. They started out with their baked specialties, which Martha wrapped in her baskets with a swirl of gossamer and ribbon. Then they stepped up production and brought in family favorites. Working intensely in their own kitchens, the women let their imaginations run wild. Audrey cooked up Italian dishes like pizza rustica and lasagna bolognese and lamb and bean stews. Every week, Vicky glazed and baked a big, juicy Virginia ham, which would then be thickly sliced for customers to take home for dinner. With the leftover ham bone, Audrey made soups—lentil, black bean, white bean, and split pea. Martha experimented with Scotch eggs—hard-boiled eggs wrapped in spicy sausage then fried until golden. Sarah invented her own chocolate-covered pound cake rabbits and to-die-for cinnamon raisin tassajara bread.

My own memory of these sweets is a dizzy haze. I recall mountains of the light, flaky palmiers—those strips of puff pastry sprinkled with sugar, folded, and caramelized. I would eat ten of those with a cup of coffee. And I remember stopping in front of the shop, startled, to see for the first time one of Martha's own seven-inch-high apple pies displayed majestically in the big window. In the days of one-inch Sara Lee frozen desserts, this pie looked like something that had landed from outer space! It certainly was the first $20 pie any of us ever bought, and once we tasted it, we could never go back to the pasty ones at the supermarket. Martha was educating our tastebuds, giving all of our palates a much-needed jolt from their slumber.

People who came into the shop were in awe of her. She'd come sweeping in with her morning stockpile, her beautiful mane of dark blond hair flying behind her, and would briskly and efficiently set up her baskets and trays in the tiny kitchen in the back. Then she would display them just so—lining the baskets with a checked napkin or lace and putting a big bow on one side or flowers and ivy entwined with the basket handle.

It was such a homespun business that at first Martha sold her main courses right in her own casserole dishes and ceramic pans and those of her team of cooks. The customers popped in to take a casserole or ham or soup home for dinner, then returned the dish the next day scrubbed clean.

Martha's formula worked—she was beginning to make a name for herself as a woman of talent and charisma who had a head for business.

When art director Corey Tippin needed a local face to pose in an ad campaign for a new Merona Sport store opening in Westport, someone suggested Martha. Corey thought, okay, ex-model, local caterer—this will be an easy one. Martha agreed to do it on the following terms: Merona Sport had to outfit her catering company in their clothing and the ad had to mention Martha's new catering company called, simply, Martha Stewart. This was a typical arrangement in the fashion business, and Merona figured it would be good publicity to have Martha's workers dressed in their clothes. After all, the clothing would get exposure at parties and events and it would be good advertising for the company. How many workers could there be? The Merona management quickly agreed to it.

At the chichi Hunt Club, a polo match was in progress—it was all very Ivy League, perfect for the shoot. Posing with another local society type, Martha is seen in the photo leaning on a split-rail fence near the polo ponies wearing a polo shirt with a matching jacket draped over her shoulder. The other model is elegantly perched on top of the fence, sidesaddle. They are both smiling directly into the camera, happy, serene, and elegant.

When the shoot wrapped, Martha and Corey struck up a conversation. "In the course of chatting, she forlornly said to me, 'I just want to get back to my farm and my chickens,'" says Corey. "The remark seemed so at odds with the shoot we had just finished that I said, 'Farm and chickens, where is your place? I want to see it.' She explained to me where she lived. Then out of the blue she asked, 'Do you want to work for me?'"

That is how Corey joined the team, at first as a bartender, then moving up the ranks to waiter, guy Friday, and party stylist—but not before witnessing this ex-fashion model get the best of his former bosses. It had never crossed any of their minds that this pretty face was once a shark on Wall Street who was no stranger to wheeling and dealing to her advantage. Soon after the photo shoot, the Merona Sport big boys were flabbergasted when they saw Martha's business deal with them unfold. Within the week, dozens of people began pouring into the new store, saying, "I work for Martha Stewart," "I work for Martha Stewart," "I work for Martha Stewart," and expecting to get fully outfitted.

"They kept coming in," Corey recalls with a laugh, "and the guys from Merona were yelling, "What's going on? Who does she think she is? *Who is this lady?*"

Through word of mouth, Martha's little market basket idea took off. Soon customers were coming into the store asking for larger and larger orders for parties and functions. Martha took quick action and expanded her team, which, in addition to her sister Laura, who baked all kinds of breads and wedding cakes, also included her brother George, who bartended, waited, and ran many of the events. George says:

We did the Shakespeare Theater in Stratford. I ran the whole concession stand. Laura worked down in the basement in the kitchen that I built for Martha, and we made picnic baskets. I was in Stratford most of the time. I had four or five people helping me. Laura was cooking the food with another woman in the basement and we ran down and picked up everything—chocolate chip cookies, chocolate-dipped strawberries. There were frittatas and mustard-crusted chicken and a couple of other dishes. It was good food. It didn't pass the health department's muster—it wasn't individually wrapped and all the other requirements—but nobody ever got sick. It was a good time.

Andy was around to help whenever he could—running errands, helping with the cleanup, and driving the vehicles.

Martha's Suburban was shared among Andy, Martha, and Corey for running errands. One time, Corey says, "While I was on a job I made all the buttons on the radio go to rock and roll and R&B stations. The next day Martha scolded me in a fun way, saying, 'Andy was so freaked out by what was on the radio every time he pushed a button.' Andy had been listening to some sort of classical Chinese music or something."

"She had a very eclectic staff," recalls Charles Case, owner of the Flower Basket in Westport, who supplied flowers for Martha's events and delivered bouquets to her house on a weekly basis. "They were all very different people, but they somehow meshed and worked together. She'd have a writer, she'd have a college student, she'd have a person just starting out and not knowing where they wanted to go. You would not normally see all these people in one room together, but they were hitting it off. It was a party within a party. Everyone had this energy that emanated from Martha and it was passed on to the clientele."

The team worked feverishly to keep up with new orders, think up new ideas, and help Martha execute the grand vision in her imagination—the most fantastic, flawless parties ever. And the team was up for it, at her beck and call.

"Martha has power over people," says Sarah. "She can get people excited about anything and everything she is doing. Just walk up to her and it will happen to you. It's not phony—it comes from this great love of life that she has."

When the women weren't cooking at home, they created in one of Martha's kitchens. She had one especially built in the basement to make the business official for local bylaw purposes. Both kitchens were dotted with dozens of little white egg timers.

Martha's house was busier than ever, people rushing in and out at all hours, racing against the buzz of the oven timers. Everybody had a job to do, even Martha's mother, who could be found at one end of the assembly line stirring a pot or two.

For the parties and events, the menu was simple American fare: corn bread and biscuits, baked beans, poached salmon, honey mustard, fresh vegetables, corn fritters, applesauce, and chocolate chip cookies. Sometimes the linens were custom-made for the event. The flowers, cut from Martha's garden when possible, were usually beautiful big bunches of irises, peonies, lilacs, or freesia.

Martha didn't just provide the food for these parties; she used her copper trays, Shaker baskets, glass cake stands, Jade-Ite, turkey platters—all the elements that were becoming her trademarks and went on to be staples of fashionable entertaining in America in the eighties and nineties. America was beginning to be comfortable as a culture with its own food and was embracing customs with less formality.

As usual, Martha's timing was impeccable. Her style was the perfect complement to the young energetic public who gave parties or attended the countless gala events that she catered.

But beyond the food and serving style, what made Martha's parties so memorable was what she did with the decor and mood. No matter how simple the fare or informal the event, Martha would think of some sort of artistic touch specific to the person or occasion.

"At Martha's parties, it was always *showtime!*" says Charles. "I think for Martha, it was like she was doing a performance."

I remember at the Cooper-Hewitt Museum in New York she elevated the crudités to the level of art when she placed sky-high mounds of blanched vegetables and fruit on the lawn of the museum like sculptures.

Then there was the opening party for the Roy Lichtenstein exhibit at the Whitney Museum, when Martha and her team airbrushed tablecloths to resemble his paintings and decorated the tables with globs of paint and other icons from his works of art, including goldfish in goblets and basketball sneakers. It was like stepping into one of his paintings.

A few days later and a few blocks away, Martha presented a harvest-themed cocktail party at the Seventh Regiment Armory that featured antique poultry cages filled with live chickens, lavender guinea fowl, and other assorted birds.

"We did a party on a pier for an antiques show and it was an autumn theme," says Corey. "George whipped together troughs of weathered wood so we could fill them with apples and such and they were a real focal point. I remember doing a party with Martha at the New York Historical Society where she built a three-tier wooden Christmas tree that fit together like a puzzle, and in between the tiers she had shelves that got smaller as they went up that were filled with food. I thought that was very clever. "

To Martha, there were no limits.

Charles Case remembers getting a breathless call from Martha from a client's home a few days before Christmas. "Charles, bring over a bunch of Christmas packages. I need to put them on a Christmas wreath—"

"But Martha, I don't have anything small enough for a wreath."

"Charles, the wreath is *very big*. Just get yourself some boxes, wrap them in colored paper and put ribbon and bows on them. *Now*."

Charles arrived at the house expecting to see Martha arranging a welcome garland on the front door. Instead, he found a mammoth six-foot wreath made of heavy grapevine and greens hanging on the living room wall. Martha had assembled the wreath from materials she found in the client's backyard. She convinced the hostess to move the dining room table into the living room under the giant wreath.

"It was wild," says Charles. "We put all the other furniture into the garage and moved the table into the living room. Along with all the place settings we put a fantastic number of candles on the table and all around the room. The aura of the candle-light was spectacular. We put little gifts on each dinner plate. I can't begin to describe the ambience created in that room."

So much of what they did was on the fly. George got a call one day from Martha saying something about an omelet party. George recalls:

"Just be here Sunday morning at eight," she told me. So I got there and she handed me a piece of paper and said, "Read this!" It was the directions for making an omelet. I read it. When we got to Fairfield Country Club, she told me I was in the kitchen and I had to cook. She said, "This is how you do it. Don't use any soap—use oil and salt to clean the pans." I tried a couple and they stuck at first, but I finally figured it out and thirty people had good omelets. That incident sparked an interest in me to cook other things.

That's how Martha is. A lot of people worked for her eight, ten years. We had fun. We learned so much and she exposed us to so much. You worked hard and at the end of the day you broke out a bottle of wine and enjoyed being tired.

The work didn't come without catastrophes, but Martha has never been the type to crumble when things go wrong. Martha is someone who can quickly transform calamity into fortune, and she tried to instill this skill in her employees.

"We had parties where something wasn't going right or an

order would come in wrong, but it was handled," says Charles. "Martha always found a solution so that it was never noticed. She never saw problems—only solutions. Once a cake tilted. Martha called me and said, 'Charles, bring some extra flowers.' We placed them around the side of the cake and no one knew anything, the cake tasted great, and no one was disappointed. During weddings, there is so much tension. The bride is understandably tense. Everything has to be perfect, which is practically impossible, and if something goes wrong it's not that you are hiding things from someone, but you want them to be happy. That's how Martha taught us to look at it—to make the people happy."

Even though she understood that to err was human, she still sought perfection. Brooke Dojny, a cook who was part of Martha's early catering team, says:

I remember at the Armory in New York City, we used these huge containers to carry everything up and down in the elevators. It was a party for three thousand people! The numbers for these parties would just boggle my mind. It all had to be packed perfectly or we wouldn't have been able to find anything.

At one cocktail party in Greenwich, Connecticut, that I was in charge of, I had forgotten the cocktail napkins. My luck, it was Sunday and of course nothing was open. I had to scrounge around the house where the party was being held and find what napkins I could. They weren't the nicest, but they were adequate. I didn't tell Martha, but someone spilled the beans. She pulled me aside and said,

"I heard you forgot the napkins." I told her that I had, but that it had worked out okay anyway. I added, and I shouldn't have, "Nobody's perfect."

Martha looked a little surprised, then said, "But we are. We have to be. That's what we aim for. *Perfection*."

It was hard sometimes to remember that everything we did had her name on it. She was not mad at us per se; she was upset at the presentation and what it might reflect.

So much of it all was about the visuals, the aesthetics, and Martha's keen eye could always detect if some detail was amiss. Brooke continues:

For Martha, there is always a right way to do things. If you cut too much off the top of the snow pea, for example, it was the wrong way. You had to take just a tiny bit off so that it wouldn't look broken. When it came to the displays of food, Martha was right in there making sure we accomplished the extraordinary portrait she saw in her mind — exactly, perfectly, and precisely.

I remember one party where the crudités — one of her masterpieces — had to be cut in a kind of interesting off-center geometric shape. At this party, whoever had peeled the carrots before they were cut and blanched had done a sloppy job and hadn't removed all the skin and you could see dark patches. Oh my God, that person would have hell to pay, but nobody would admit who did it. I think we all just kind of tucked our heads into our chests and scuttled off. Whoever did that never did it again.

Let's be honest, Martha's creativity is inspiring for everyone. I think some may have perhaps forgotten how being around Martha enabled them to do what they did so well. She inspired everyone to produce their best and somehow she magically instilled in us all a passion for our daily work routines.

In retrospect, many of her coworkers want to believe that it all came from their own talents and they forget the collaborative aspects Martha brought to the mix. It was her perfectionism that drove you to do your utmost to meet her standards. That was what you were being paid for. It was very exciting being in that kitchen, at that time, and part of that creative process.

As every hostess knows, no matter what the catastrophe, you don't let them see you sweat. And in Martha's case, you present a pretty face—even if you've been up since four A.M. feeding the chickens and dicing the carrots.

At a party Martha planned and catered for the launch of the book *Gnomes*, published to massive success by Andy, who was now running the publishing company Abrams, the team started at dawn and was setting up until the very last possible moment.

"I remember seeing Martha that day. She had wound up her hair with little ribbons all over," recalls Corey, "and she wore a cap over that and she had on a blue jumpsuit, like an automobile mechanic wears. The whole place was being decorated with pine trees and satchels. It was very nicely done. She even talked some parents into letting little girls lie under the foliage as little fairies and such. And as the party began, Martha pulled all the ribbons out of her hair. It made a kind of chic crinkly look. Then she zipped off her blue jumpsuit and underneath it she had on a black party dress and she was ready to roll. All day she had been dressed like that and no one knew it. She looked really great. I thought, if you can do this work and just unzip and step out like a butterfly emerging from a cocoon, now *that's* style!"

That kind of style took organization and know-how, Martha told her team. Whether it was how to wash the floor, cut the beans, or pour cream from the carton, there was a proper, organized way to do things, to be efficient, and to avoid waste.

"When you pour cream," Martha instructed the cooks, "set the carton back down and wait five minutes. This allows the thick cream time to run back down the sides to the bottom of the container."

The cooks shook their heads in disbelief but they did as instructed because Martha knew best. Think of all that cream you'd be wasting if you didn't do it! In the catering business, multiply one hundred cartons times one tablespoon—in the kitchen, frugality was a must, and every ingredient was utilized to its maximum potential.

Martha didn't ask her staff to do anything she wouldn't do herself. "If you didn't clean something properly, she would bark at you but be cleaning at the same time," Sarah says. "Not only the KitchenAid but the floor. She could be down on the floor cleaning while she complained that you were not keeping it clean. Always clean up after yourself—that was one of her mottoes and it's not a bad one. It's having respect for your work environment, caring for what you are doing and she is doing. We'd be working our butts off in her kitchen, but she'd be right there behind you helping and cleaning up, washing the floor and the counters and the pots and pans. She could be a tyrant, but she was right there with us all the way."

As for Martha's so-called "barking," many people have commented on it, but I think it's almost a genetic thing. Her sisters have the same deep-voiced, brisk way of talking—if you heard her sister Laura on the phone, you'd swear it was Martha. Martha's dad had always coached the kids "from the diaphragm, from the gut"—they were trained like actors whose voices have to reach the rafters. Combine that with the family's very no-nonsense manner, and Martha may often have sounded harsh when she didn't really mean it that way.

Sarah says, "She would be furious over nonperfection, like overcooking green beans—the fine line between overcooking and not overcooking green beans or asparagus and keeping the color was huge in Martha's world and very hard to teach. Green beans can be a bitch to cook and actually remain green. Sometimes they turn that horrible yellow—I don't use them if that happens and Martha would *never*. We'd have to buy more. All this was about taking responsibility for what you do—was it your responsibility or was Martha to take all the responsibility?"

Martha was a tough teacher, but often those are the people who teach us the most, as the women who worked with her attest. Audrey says:

Once Martha called me at six o'clock at night to tell me she was catering a brunch the next day for ten people and needed spanakopita, the Greek spinach pies that are extremely time consuming to make. I said, "How am I going to make them? The stores are closed. Where can I find the time for that?" She got snippy and said, "Well, I'll just do them myself." Then I thought, by God, if she can do it, then I could. That is the life of a caterer. In her own way, she pushed me into doing things I never dreamed I could do. The next thing I knew, I was providing food for Paul Newman's daughter's sixteenth birthday party, I was cooking for Jack Paar, and Janis Ian was requesting an order of my pecan bars to take along on one of her concert tours.

Martha was brilliant at generating publicity. She took four of us with her to be on a popular radio show, *The Pat McCann Show*, and I remember being terrified. When Pat turned to me and said, "I hear you are the famous thumb cookie lady," I went deaf, dumb, and blind. I stammered, "I've got big thumbs!"

I knew very early on what Martha was like to work with—notice I say "work with" and not "work for." It was a collaboration. I had to tell people all the time—I still find myself doing so to this day—when they would ask, "What was she like to work with? She's a bitch, right?" I told them no way! She is not like you and she is not like me. She's not going to get on the phone at seven in the morning and gossip and chat. She has an agenda. And boy, what an agenda! But so does every male CEO in this country who built their companies from scratch.

"If you watched Martha at a party you might think she was being overly fastidious," says Charles, "but in the end you realize that it made a difference. When there was something you thought no one would notice, you would hear word back that the way the napkins were folded were a real hit or the lighting was what made the party. Martha never overlooked those pesky little details."

That kind of focus, say her coworkers, helped to inspire the creativity. "All of her adamant obsessive behavior about being organized or having everything in the right place or keeping things clean and neat, that feeds creativity," says Sarah, looking back on those days. "I've really grown to appreciate that part of it all."

So have I.

5

Mentoring

Working too hard will never kill you. It's the food, drinking, and other vices that will do you in.

—MARTHA STEWART

S ome of Martha's employees were young women who had no skills in the workplace. Working with her was like boot camp in how to start and run a business. Everyone within earshot of Martha when she was on the phone talking money with clients was in on the dynamics of her impressive negotiating skills. Whether her cooks knew it or not, they were witness to a small piece of what Martha Stewart the businesswoman was all about. Many of her employees tell me that it was only years later when they had to utilize some of the same techniques in their own businesses that they realized what Martha had taught them.

Many of these women—some divorced and raising children on their own—told me it was a godsend to be able to work at home, be close to their children, and not have to find a job in an office or a store. They are unanimous in appreciating the opportunity Martha offered them.

"I noticed in the beginning that what Martha was doing was elevating what women do all the time and saying it didn't have to be all drudgery," says Vicky Sloat, one of Martha's former assistants. "It was good. It was honoring women's work and that was an incredible thing. It was not just women's work that she transformed with her imagination, though; it was all of life in general. We all can't do it at the level that Martha does it, but that's not the point. She's the example, she's the artist and the inspiration."

Martha's housekeeper, Necy Fernandez, took inspiration from the Big Boss and quickly moved up in the ranks of the family business. "I started working for her cleaning the house once a week," says Necy, "but Martha would vacuum her house in the middle of the night and she was always washing her floors. One time I got to her house in the morning and the basement was all clean and organized. Martha had been up cleaning since three o'clock in the morning. The first week I was there she asked me if I wanted to work weekends in the catering business. We started to get real busy and so I had to get somebody else to help her clean the house."

When Martha began giving lunchtime seminars, teaching women about party planning, Necy helped her set up and set the tables. And as is often the case with Martha, you learned on the job and you learned fast. "She used to do all the tables, then once she stopped and left all the tables for me to do and I thought, 'Oh my God, I have to do this all myself?' This is how I started. I always loved flowers. I used to finish cleaning her house and then would go in the garden and cut the flowers and put them in her house. Andy would say, 'Now Necy, I'm so confused—I don't know which flowers are yours and which flowers are Martha's! This vase is my wife's, right?' And I would laugh and say, 'No, this one is me!' Then Martha said, 'Necy, go to Paul Newman's house and do the flowers.' She pushed me to the point where I had to learn it. She taught me to do everything."

Necy took Martha's varied moods in stride and knew that Martha always regretted her outbursts, even if she could not articulate it in the way people wanted her to. She explains:

> She was always very nice to me, very nice. There were times when she screamed or was really mad. She would always call me the next day to see if I was mad or not. This is her way. She never would say, "I'm sorry." But calling is her way to apologize. Doing something to make you feel better, but never apologizing—that is not Martha's way.
>
> There are a lot of things she's done that I admire her so much for. I have a friend, Lara, who came here thirty-five years ago. Martha hired her to do her housecleaning, and she was a little sick by this time and had trouble hearing. She got worse and worse and then she got really bad. Martha, with all the money she had, could have afforded to pay someone who hears and could do the job, but she kept Lara all those years. The fact that she did that makes me feel good about her.
>
> So many friends and most of my brothers and sisters have worked for Martha. Everyone who came from Brazil who didn't have a job, Martha hired them.

At age nineteen Vicky Sloat was a mere ninety pounds. Martha patiently took her under her wing as her assistant to teach her about food and, in the process, about her own strengths.

"I was very fragile and struggling with eating," says Vicky, now a mother and homemaker. "Martha taught me and disciplined me with a kind heart. In a loving and nurturing way, she brought me back to life."

As far as personalities go, you couldn't find two people more different than Vicky and Martha. Vicky was the kind to burst into tears at the drop of a spoon. Martha was just the firm hand she needed and was willing to work with Vicky, teaching her how to do the smallest tasks.

One day at the supermarket, Vicky got a dose of Martha's tough love. They had packed the groceries for that day's cooking into the trunk. Instead of putting the shopping cart back safely to the side in the parking lot, Vicky gave the cart a haphazard little shove.

Martha was horrified. "Don't just throw your shopping cart— you can't let it go flying into the parking lot!" Martha scolded her, then pulled her aside and in a softer voice, explained. "Listen, Vicky, you have to park it. That's not considerate of other people."

"What she was really saying to me," Vicky says with emotion in her voice, "was 'Pay attention. *Snap out of it.*' I was in my own world and she brought me out of it."

Martha took note of Vicky's hidden talents and brought them to the surface. Vicky had been handwriting the place cards for many of Martha's parties using her unique, rather eccentric calligraphy. When Andy had begun work on publishing *Gnomes*, a collection of drawings of "little people," Martha saw in her mind's eye Vicky's spidery handwriting on the pages of the book and gave Andy one of her firm urgings—"Andy, you simply *must* use Vicky's handwriting!" He promptly commissioned Vicky to do the job.

There were tender moments. Martha was not the type to cry with a friend and smother her with kisses and hugs. She had her own subtle ways that showed she had you in her heart. After one particularly trying day that ended with Vicky in tears, Martha handed her a handkerchief, took her out back to the henhouse, and pointed out the beautiful blue and green Araucana eggs that her coveted birds had laid. She held the delicate eggs in her hand and showed them to Vicky, who felt Martha was silently saying that they are born with a fragile shell only to hatch into a beautiful bird that will soon soar through the sky.

The mere fact that Martha trusted and depended on her made Vicky want to improve herself. "Martha gave me the confidence to be able to do things on my own. Later on I did some catering and I taught cooking classes for children after school."

Vicky is now married with six children and is still living in Westport. She credits Martha for turning her once-desperate world around.

"I remember my times with Martha and the playfulness and pleasures of her world—her creativity, and all the beauty, and how whimsical and fanciful she is. As I wash the dishes today and wipe off the counter for the millionth time, I remember Martha's inspiration. I'll go and get some more pots, beautiful ones, and bring my plants in for the winter. When all the washing and cooking becomes tiring and dull, I can be revived by the pleasures of Martha's world."

In 2003, twenty years after leaving her employ, Vicky ran into Martha at a local organic market. They gave each other a big hug, and the first thing out of Martha's mouth were words of caring that Vicky was healthy: "Vicky, you are still eating, aren't you?"

At the time Louise Felix was pulled into Martha's galaxy, she also needed a strong, positive influence. "I was drinking a lot. Working for Martha helped me get over that because I would be put in situations where I would drink like a fish and she would call me on it."

After one breakfast event that Louise and Corey Tippin helped Martha with in Manhattan, the three were driving back to Westport after being up since four A.M. "Corey and I were like two zombies in the backseat of Martha's car, suckling on bottles of champagne and eating chocolate chip cookies. There was so much sugar infused in our systems. This was on the way back from the city, and I'm thinking I had never done that in my history of drinking and drugging. But Martha was great about it. We were scolded and simply told to never do it again. Quite frankly, in many ways she brought me to a place where I could see what I was doing to myself. She saw me heading for trouble and said to me, 'I don't know what you expect out of me, Louise, but there's just so much I can do.' That alone was enough for me to take a look at myself. I didn't realize how great my problem had become, but she was very aware of it. Listen, we all have our stories of bizarre moments with Martha, but I challenge anyone who can't say the same about their own family."

Many years later, after Louise became successful in her own business in the eyewear trade, she spotted Martha on the street. "I went up to her and said, 'My God, your patience with me was worth so much. Thank you.' And she said, 'Don't worry about it, Louise, we're all human.' She was so gracious."

Martha was a woman who was turning "woman's work" into a savvy business any CEO would be jealous of. Within the first year, the business snowballed.

"We were all caught up in the excitement that swirled around Martha," says Brooke Dojny. "I am sure she had hired me with the intention of allowing me a flexible schedule, but when the levee broke, she had only a very few to pick up the slack. We worked at a frenetic pace and were giddy from the exhaustion. If we didn't know it, we felt it; Martha was headed for the stars."

To keep up with the pace, razor-sharp scheduling was a daily routine, and deadlines loomed larger and larger. "Operate beyond all normal limits!" became Martha's rallying cry to her troops. To Martha, there was no other way to work. Stay focused, but multitask to the max. Drink ample amounts of coffee if you couldn't keep up with her. If you partied all night, that was your problem.

The days were long, and for Martha, the leader of the pack, they were the longest. I think she was one of those people who hardly needed sleep. She would either be up until three A.M. icing a wedding cake or she'd get up in the wee hours—four A.M. or so—and start preparations while the others would roll in at Turkey Hill "late" at sunrise. Audrey Doneger says:

I remember being up all night worrying about my fifteen-year-old daughter. She was having a tough time and driving me up the wall. And I thought, I'm up. I might as well cook! So I decided to deliver the goods to Martha at four in the morning. Everyone knew that Martha would be up. When I arrived, Martha was in the garden. I can't explain it, but she looked like she stepped off the pages of a magazine. She was out there in her yard gathering eggs. I was amazed.

We eventually made our way back into the house. We sat down in the kitchen and waited for something to come out of the oven. I started unloading about my daughter, Suzie, saying, "You know—remember what it was like to be an adolescent?"

And I remember this like it was yesterday. Martha's face went blank and she looked me square in the face and said, "No, I never went through that. I was always too busy."

I tried again. "You know, the pimply, awkward stage . . ."

She said, "No, I didn't go through that."

At first, I must have given her an incredulous stare, but then it dawned on me: she had this certain kind of disposition that only comes from beauty—and I really don't think she did.

It was odd when the women who were working so hard creaming their butter and stirring their soups so they could build a solid business to be proud of got grief from the local planning and zoning commission and the health department.

"The health officials showed up at the Market Basket," recalls

Sarah Gross. "They questioned us. They were sitting watching us come and go and wanted to know where we were cooking our food. This was even before Martha had her kitchen down in the basement, and we were all cooking out of our homes. We weren't even cooking at Martha's. It was part of the group effort to make it a success; it was part of the whole allure—sneaking around and doing this great thing, a great concept and getting away with it."

As soon as they began doing the bulk of the cooking at Turkey Hill, it was the nosy neighbors' turn to cry foul. "The neighbors were always complaining because we were usually cleaning up in the wee hours of the morning," says Corey Tippin. "The kitchen was a long narrow cellar where we did the baking, cooking, dishwashing, everything. It was only about eight feet by twenty-five feet with a low, low ceiling. The cooking and preparing began early in the morning and went on until four in the afternoon. Then the intricate packing of Martha's Suburban would begin. We'd be back at some awful hour, and then the cleanup would begin. The neighbors were never happy with the scene, because by this time we were a truly rambunctious bunch, clattering the pots and pans, laughing and yelling— Martha right along with us."

And so the war began—the town of Westport versus Martha, who had always tried to keep good relations with the other families on her street. "She bent over backward to keep the neighbors happy," say Max and Loretta Bernegger, who lived two doors down from Turkey Hill, "but of course there was always one who was nosy and made trouble for her. She sent plants to the neighbors and invited neighbors over. If the garden was in full bloom, she invited everyone over for a walk in the garden. And she gave the most fantastic Christmas parties for all her neighbors and friends—the house was left wide open to them! Of course, she was hard-working and hard-nosed—she had to be, with the business she was in and to be where she is today— you have to be pretty tough. Tough for a man is great. Tough for a woman, she's a bitch. That is what they said about her from the beginning."

A few applauded Martha's entrepreneurial spirit, but others saw her as a nuisance. This was something I could never understand about Westport, a town built by bohemians and artists. If you stroll along the entrance to Compo Beach, you'll see a bronze statue of a Revolutionary War soldier kneeling on the ground (it was immortalized in a famous *I Love Lucy* episode); the town of Westport celebrates its rebels! But not Martha. Apparently her revolution was not worth much to them, even though she employed its citizens and created splendor around them.

To me, Martha was a true artist and warrior of mythical proportions. Back then, when I would wander into any of Martha's kitchens as the women worked away on the flour-dusted countertops, I would think that even her garbage looked like something you'd find on a painter's easel. In one galvanized garbage can, you'd see an explosion of colors—tightly tied throngs of lily of the valley, plump pink peonies, sun-faced daisies mixed with lavender wisteria and foxglove. The garbage can next to that would be brimming with organic shrapnel—skins from cored and scored apples, peach pits, broccoli florets, and peeled potatoes.

Martha would fight many battles besides the one with the town of Westport. But this was an especially painful one for

Martha because she lost many friends in the process. Even after she acquired the proper permits and had moved much of her business to a commercial space, the neighbors still tried to stall her efforts. They simply didn't understand her. I, in turn, did not understand them. But she did not let them stop her. Martha always believed nothing was insurmountable and that when an opportunity comes your way, it was put in front of you for a reason.

Martha continued to grab opportunities with gusto. The busier her team got, the higher the stress, the more they all blew off steam in the kitchen, especially Martha. It was true that if she was not in a great mood, her words could sting. But she usually meant nothing by it.

"The thing about Martha is that she does not mince words," says her brother George. "So if she doesn't like something, she'll tell you exactly what's wrong with it and make you feel like crap for doing it. She's not very diplomatic in a lot of instances."

One problem with battle is that the troops get tired and worn down, and some of Martha's best soldiers were getting weary under the pressures. Brooke Dojny recalls:

> Usually she was very, very fair, but still, you know, it can really be hard on the ego. She wouldn't micromanage you unless you were screwing up badly. There were a couple of times when she lost her temper with me. It was a bit scary. I think that we were all under so much stress because the business just took off. There were so many parties, so much going on, and so little space in her house to get all this work completed. And when people had to put in eighteen-hour days, nerves were frayed.

It was about this time that I thought I should move on. I mean, her list of weddings in June of that year was so long it was positively frightening. I thought, how could we possibly get them done? I just couldn't imagine being there because I still had two young children at home and I wanted to see them! I guess I was just getting burnt out. It was hard to keep up with Martha's pace. She has the endurance of a long-distance runner.

Then she started to plan her brother George's wedding. The whole wedding, top to bottom, was to be photographed and involved many separate photo shoots with many set-ups within those shoots. For most people, a wedding is an extremely daunting task, and occasionally it becomes someone's full-time job. But not for Martha. She could handle it and then some.

Martha ran faster than anyone else, perhaps because she knew where the road was leading. Corey recalls driving in the car with Martha and the rest of the gang one day. Martha recognized someone in the car next to them. "She said, 'There goes that TV producer. He wants to do a sitcom based on my life and our catering business called *Food*.' Well, we all started laughing, but she was serious. And then she said, 'I want Candice Bergen to play me.' I thought, why the hell not? Anything was possible. This was Martha. She had the will and a way to get whatever she wanted."

The race was never over—it never slowed down, and, in fact, it increased with alarming speed. Martha was the first to admit that she liked operating on the edge and jumping over that edge gave her heightened clarity. It motivated her, got her juices flowing.

. . .

When Martha got her first book deal, for *Entertaining*, the work doubled in intensity. Martha asked all her employees to write out their favorite recipes so she could include them in the book. George says:

> People don't know that it took three years to make that book and during that time every single plate and every platter that left every party was photographed. Everything had to be perfectly designed and laid out and either a professional photographer was there or Andy was there with his camera. Martha had boxes and boxes of negatives. Martha would have competitions in the kitchens for who could do the best crudité platters.
>
> All the women went overboard and designed these massive things. While it was excruciatingly hard work, it was fun, and most of them loved one another; most had a great time. Some people were disappointed, but they came in with big egos. These people would come to work for Martha, come in on fire and then go whizzing off and burnt out with nothing to show for it except recognition in this book or that book. They'd claim she was stealing ideas and doing this and that, but they were fully aware of what was happening. It's just like any other kitchen. If you look at big fancy restaurants in Manhattan, who gets the recognition? The head chef.
>
> Anyone who works at a corporation understands that whatever work he does, whatever ideas she comes up with,

belong to the corporation. If you work for Microsoft and you have an idea, who gets the credit? Bill Gates. That was the case with Martha, too.

If you look at all the opulence that we tried to create, especially at the Cooper-Hewitt, when we could make those huge mounds of color, blueberries and strawberries and this and that with all the vegetables mixed, in and then when you looked around afterward, everyone was copying it. Does she get credit? Mostly she gets criticism. People think she's stolen everything she's ever done, but you can't be as successful as she is and not have ideas of your own. Come on! Her creativity is just phenomenal and she feeds everyone's creativity. That's not to say she hasn't hired talented people. She has, but she knows how to get them to create more than they ever thought they had in themselves.

Lexi also supports her mother on this topic. "My mother has always gathered recipes, ideas, skills, and information and passed them on to anyone who has the interest to learn. Practically everyone who gave my mother an idea or even a recipe throughout the years got credit; the few that didn't still bad-mouth her to this day. Where'd they get the recipe, anyway? Don't tell me they made it up. *Please*.

"Mom believes in giving credit, but when it comes to a publication, she also believes it has to be balanced for the sake of structure and feel of the book or magazine. Everything is taken into account in publishing. It's beyond me how anyone could feel possessive about a simple recipe."

Audrey, Martha's "Cookie Lady of Westport," saw the bigger

picture as well. After her lemon squares became a success, she developed a pecan bar that she baked in huge pans; it became a big hit. Both cookie recipes were included in Martha's book, *Entertaining*. "People said to me, 'She's stealing your recipe! How can you let her get away with this?' But to me, that's like saying someone is stealing your joke. What are there, five jokes in the whole world? Every other joke is a variation. My recipes aren't secret. Anyone who wants a recipe, I give it to them. It wasn't my original idea, anyway. Martha made her own lemon bar and put her own tweak on it. And she made them taste better. If she didn't know a certain dish, she would go out and get the best person known for that specialty to teach her how to do it. And then she did it better than they ever did."

Martha is special like an artist, and when you throw in an intellect that is off the charts, you get someone who may not act quite like the rest of us. Get ordinariness out of your head when you think of Martha; she is not wired that way. Some of her hard workers, though, perhaps needed to hear a few ordinary words that are so easy for others to say and were so hard to come by in Martha's kitchen.

"Once there was this little note in her little handwriting thanking me after I worked my butt off," Sarah Gross recalls. "It said 'thank you' and I cried because it was so rare for that to happen. I think it even said 'Love, Martha.'"

When Martha was putting together stories for her book *Weddings*, she called wedding planner Renny Reynolds to see what high-class wedding she could photograph for the book. Famed for creating events at Studio 54 and parties for Bianca Jagger, Elizabeth Taylor, and Dolly Parton, Renny was known in society circles for being the one to call for understated good taste. Martha had already photographed one wedding he had worked on in Dallas, and had just found out about another one he was doing in Virginia, and she asked if she could include that one in her book as well. This time he told her no, that the clients were very private.

The day of the wedding, "It was a very warm spring day, much warmer than usual," Renny recalls. "We had just planted the gardens with hundreds of tulips. I was on a ladder trying to apply a decorative floral trim over the front door when out of the corner of my eye I saw a couple walking up the drive. This was a very long drive so I couldn't tell at first who it was, but as they approached I realized it was Martha and Andy. This was in the middle of the boondocks and there was no way they could have just have been in the area and casually come upon the house. I lost it completely—Martha's not the only one with a temper. I jumped off the ladder and laid into her with a vengeance. I was screaming as I jumped down from the ladder and I informed her in so many four-letter words that she was to get off the property. I scared the hell out of both of them. She had really pushed me to my limit, and I didn't need it on that day."

Omar Honeyman, one of Martha's employees, remembers Martha crashing another wedding for the sake of her book:

I had mentioned to the caterer at the time that this would be a great thing for Martha Stewart to know about for her book, and he said, "Oh, you don't tell her *anything*. Don't you *ever* tell her anything about this." And I thought, why should he decide this? Why shouldn't the bride be the one to decide this?

I called Martha and I said, "Martha, there is a wedding going to take place, and the Greyhound bus is going to take everyone over to the waterfront and put them on a yacht." Martha said, "Oh, that sounds great" and I told her, "But you can't let anyone know you found this out from me."

Martha showed up and she went into the house with her photographer and a guy with a big white umbrella to take pictures of everything, although she had nothing to do with any of it. A lot of people asked, "Who is that woman?" It ended up being one of the chapters in her book!

When Corey came on board, he had already worked with some of the biggest names in the art and fashion worlds, such as Andy Warhol and Karl Lagerfeld, so he was no stranger to a demanding boss. "I understand Martha," he says. "I understand her behavior and I accept it. I excuse the difficult parts because there is so much more to her. You really have to understand the dynamic and the near insanity of being that brilliant to really get a handle on Martha."

But even Corey wilted under the intense heat Martha could turn up high. When the two were planning a party for the actress Pia Zadora, Corey says:

I was thinking up all these ideas for the party, you know, really crazy stuff to do: scarecrows made out of mops and brooms with white garden gloves stuffed with straw to act as

Pia's backup singers. I had asked Martha what the budget was because I needed to know what I could purchase for the party.

And she barked back, "What do you mean, what's the budget?"

I answered, sarcastically, "You know, how much do we get, and how much do you want to spend?"

"That's no concern of yours!" she yelled.

Well, of course that led to a huge fight. It had been building up for some time, and we just snapped and said awful things to each other. I finally walked.

"You know what, Martha? Just do it yourself!" I told her. And I walked out. And that was that. For years I didn't see Martha. She tried to contact me, she tried to make up, she tried to be nice. She made overtures to be friends again, but I was a jerk and I just wasn't able to do it at that time in my life.

Corey always felt Martha held back emotionally on the friendship front:

I remember this very giddy and young side of Martha. It's still there today and it continues to drive her.

One Sunday years ago, I went over to Turkey Hill. I had to stop by and there she was with Lexi; they were laughing and running and Martha looked like Lexi's sister; freshly scrubbed and with her hair down. I felt slightly uncomfortable, intruding on their private Sunday morning. I was struck with a sense of longing to have such an intimate moment in my life and a sense of loss of not being that close to her.

I began to understand that Martha provokes this longing in people. They want to get close to her, but that can never be. She's her own person—a private person—and that's the way it is.

When Martha's wildly successful coffee-table book *Entertaining* came out in the early eighties, the national news services decided to poke their noses into Martha's business. The charges were picayune—a recipe that was not credited, a recipe that didn't work. The final charge. Martha was a showoff.

After several years, Sarah, too, parted ways with Martha after they had spent so much time in the trenches together. "She was ferocious—but for a reason I only understand now," Sarah says.

Today, Sarah has her own catering business and says she is blessed with a staff that understands her own ferocity as a leader. "I laugh sometimes about how I get, and I feel as though I'm becoming more like Martha every day in how demanding I can be," she says. "Martha sets such a high standard for people to live up to and 99 percent of the time they aren't there, so when people don't get there, when they don't make the mark, it is incredibly frustrating for her. I've only recently come to this realization because of what I now expect from others. I understand Martha's impatience now. People weren't moving at her pace and it was driving her crazy."

Back then, though, Sarah did not understand this. She had been running the catering business at full speed, was making a minimal hourly wage, and was feeling underappreciated. She got up the nerve to approach Martha and give her an ultimatum: she wanted a title and a piece of the action or she was getting out of the kitchen.

"I didn't realize how ballsy that was of me to ask," she says. Even ballsier was the response she got, one that Sarah will never forget. What Martha was heading for had nothing to do with chance and everything to do with a pure intention and an unequivocally clear picture of the future.

"Andy was in the room," Sarah recalls. He turned to Sarah and in the most matter-of-fact manner said to her: "You know, Martha is going to be as big as McDonald's. *And we're not going to give any of it away.*"

Martha's father, Edward Kostyra.
(Courtesy of Martha Kostyra)

The Kostyra family. In the back row, from left: Frank, Martha, and Eric; in the front row, from left: Kathy, baby Laura, Martha Sr. (or "Big Martha," as she is affectionately called), Edward, and George. *(Courtesy of Martha Kostyra)*

Martha's sister Kathy and Mrs. Kostyra in their Nutley, New Jersey, kitchen in a snapshot taken by Martha's father. *(Courtesy of Martha Kostyra)*

Martha and Laura at Kathy's wedding. *(Courtesy of Laura Plimpton)*

Martha's daughter, Alexis (or Lexi, as she is called), at eleven years old. *(Courtesy of Laura Plimpton)*

Publishing veteran Gerry Gross and Martha at the Cooper-Hewitt in New York City in June 1976. *(Courtesy of Gerry Gross and* Publishers Weekly*)*

Beverly's Collectibles, one of Martha's early haunts, where she often looked for valuable old finds. Martha loves flea markets and tag sales and goes to them whenever she can. *(Photograph by Stewart Bronfeld)*

Some of Martha's prized hens in Westport, Connecticut. *(Courtesy of Judy Morris)*

Martha's siblings Laura and George among Martha's sunflowers in the late seventies. *(Courtesy of Laura Plimpton)*

Andy Stewart (right) and an unidentified man at the book party for *Faeries*.
(Courtesy of Laura Plimpton)

Audrey Doneger while on vacation in Venice. She was one of the first women to work for Martha's catering business and later became famous for her lemon square recipe. *(Photograph by Audrey's daughter Susan Pujalte)*

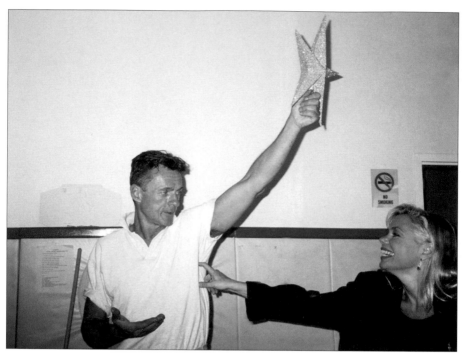

Corey Tippin holding up a star that he made for Martha. *(Courtesy of Judy Morris)*

Vicky Sloat, one of Martha's assistants. When Vicky had her first baby, Martha paid her a visit and gave her a one-year subscription to the Toy of the Month Club. *(Photograph by Vicky Sloat's husband, Bob Sloat)*

Martha holding Judy Morris's baby, Jimmy. *(Courtesy of Judy Morris)*

Martha invited two of her longtime employees, Carolyn Kelly-Wallach and Lisa Wagner, and their sons (from left, Ethan Goldberg, Gregory Kelly-Wallach, and Alexander Goldberg) to stay with her at her house in Maine. *(Photograph by Carolyn's husband, Barry Wallach)*

Martha dancing with one of her employees, John Hanson. *(Courtesy of John Hanson)*

Martha in the Clinton White House. At top, Martha and First Lady Hillary Rodham Clinton. *(Courtesy of Judy Morris)* At bottom, Martha and Mrs. Clinton among friends and colleagues. Judy Morris is at the far left. *(Official White House photograph)*

Martha with, from left, Michael Bolton, John Kerry, and Paul Newman at a party. *(Author's collection)*

Martha and her team holding Emmys won for her TV show *Martha Stewart Living* after the awards ceremony. *(Official Emmys photograph)*

The Papaya King, Martha's favorite spot to grab a delicious hot dog when she's in Manhattan. *(Photograph by Natasha Stoynoff)*

Callen Pappy, the eleven-year-old granddaughter of Jeanne Pappy, a fan who spotted Martha in the New York Marriott Marquis in 1999 and asked for a photo. Martha stopped for the picture and has kept in touch with them ever since. *(Photograph by Jeanne Pappy)*

Martha with her friend and talented hairstylist Eva Scrivo. *(Photograph by Vanessa Lenz)*

Photographers waiting for Martha to exit the court-house during her trial. *(Photograph by Sophie Herbert)*

One of Martha's many fans expressing his affection for Martha and his distaste for the courtroom proceedings. *(Photograph by Sophie Herbert)*

The train station in Alderson, West Virginia, the town where Martha was incarcerated. (Photograph by Lloyd Allen)

Betty Alderson, who owns a shop in the town named after her family, holding a T-shirt she had made up in honor of Martha. (Photograph by Betty Alderson's husband, John Alderson IV)

Martha, her brother George, and their mother at a dinner celebrating George's fiftieth birthday. *(Courtesy of George Kostyra)*

The cake Martha baked for her mother's ninetieth birthday party. *(Courtesy of Martha Kostyra)*

Big Martha sitting proudly at her ninetieth birthday party, happily surrounded by her family. From left: Laura Plimpton, George Christiansen, Kathy Evans, Martha, and Laura's husband, Randy. *(Courtesy of Martha Kostyra)*

Alexis Stewart in the fall of 2005. *(Courtesy of Alexis Stewart)*

Inside Martha's studio for her daily show, *Martha*, at the end of the show when Martha takes questions from the audience and when photo taking is allowed. *(Author's collection)*

The exterior and entrance to Martha's new studio on West 26th Street in New York City, showing posters promoting the show as well as *Martha Stewart Living*. *(Author's collection)*

Martha and her beloved mother, Martha Kostyra. *(Courtesy of Martha Kostyra)*

6

Doing Everything

There was nothing else on television
that looked like that.

—LISA WAGNER

M artha Stewart has been branded a lot of nasty names—most of all the overused b-word. One day when she was doing a television appearance, one of her hairstylists, Kelly, was wearing a novelty T-shirt. Kelly rushed up to Martha to give her hair a quick spritz as the cameras began to roll. Martha looked at Kelly's T-shirt and burst out laughing. She stopped the cameras and called over a photographer, then insisted that Kelly pose with her in a photo for her Web site. Martha put her arm around Kelly, and, as the photographer snapped away, she proudly displayed Kelly's T-shirt, on the front of which, in big, bold letters, were the words I WANT TO BE MARTHA STEWART BECAUSE THE BITCH CAN DO EVERYTHING.

"It was such a great thing," says John Hanson, who worked for Martha. "Every now and then we would bring in these parody books like *Martha Stewart's Better Than You Are at Entertaining*, *Is Martha Stewart Living?* and *Martha Stewart's Excruciatingly Perfect Weddings*, and she loved all that stuff, because to her it was the sincerest form of flattery. She loved the *Saturday Night Live* parodies as well. She didn't take it seriously."

Nasty names didn't bother Martha one bit. Her successes were swirling about her, so what did she care? She had other worries—namely, her husband. After his grand prediction about their future success together, both Martha and Lexi were blindsided by Andy Stewart's decision to leave his wife in 1987 and pursue a relationship with one of Martha's assistants, Robyn.

"Many think she let her work interfere too much with her marriage," says Martha's mother. Her brother George has other explanations:

> Martha used to have migraines. I remember her saying, "I can't believe it. I've had this headache for *four weeks*." It was incessant. Physically, she was climbing the walls. I think that was one of the reasons Andy was driven away. She was just in constant excruciating pain.
>
> Then there's the fine line between love and hate and all the things that happen in a relationship. One minute you wake up and you kiss someone good morning and in the next moment you're screaming at them or they're screaming at you. Things are coming at you from all sides from many fronts. You go literally insane.
>
> I think Martha has probably been there and back many, many times, but look at the stakes she's got. They're bigger than anything we'll ever see, that's for sure.

One thing all friends and family will attest to is that even though Martha has never been one to put her heart on her sleeve—she didn't speak of Andy at all after he left—it was obvious she was in pain.

"It was very tough on her when Andy left," says Necy Fernandez, "very tough. She was very surprised, and she loved him, I know that. I was the one person who was always around them. The only time I saw Martha crying was when he left her. He was very sad, too. Andy was the type of man who needs time for himself and most of the time Martha kept him so busy."

Sarah Gross also saw the deep sadness in Martha. She had left Martha's employment the day Andy made his fateful big-as-McDonald's speech but had since patched things up with Martha. She started her own catering business, and had been hired by Martha to do some catering.

Sarah was excited to be back at Turkey Hill. "I took a walk around the gardens," she says, "and everything looked really different to me. I had had this magical picture of what it was like back when I was eighteen, nineteen years old. But now it felt so different. The garden felt overgrown—it just felt kind of mangled. It was a surreal experience to go back years later, after not being there at all. I said to Martha how different everything looked, and she looked at me and said, 'Well, Sarah, that's the evolution of a garden.'"

Martha walked back into the house, and Sarah stood still for a few moments before getting back into her van. "I drove away and started crying," says Sarah. "I saw this inner sadness and emptiness in Martha. The outside was looking great—she had created this experience around her—but on the inside there seemed to be a void."

Some friends take a tougher view of Martha's tears. "Sure,

Martha was surprised when Andy left," says one friend. "Martha lost something. She doesn't like to lose anything. And she lost big-time. But I think the divorce was the real catalyst that pushed Martha and Lexi together. I think they both needed each other terribly."

Meanwhile, Andy took an apartment in Manhattan in the West Village, a few blocks from Omar Honeyman. "It was a cute, tiny apartment," says Omar, who bumped into Andy soon after Andy moved in. "I asked how Lexi was. He said, 'I don't know; we don't talk much.'"

It didn't take long for Martha to approach the divorce with businesslike briskness—at least on the outside. Corey Tippin remembers:

> She'd walk through the kitchen, holding papers in her hands having to do with Andy and their separation, the divorce papers, saying, *"Corey, look at this*! Look what he wants from me now!" I was supersensitive about it because I had just broken up with my partner after a long relationship. I was a wreck and I felt like I was literally going crazy. I was going around moaning, "How long am I going to be in pain? I'm losing my mind. What am I going to do?"
>
> Martha was going through her pain, too, but she came up to me and stuck her finger on my chest and said, "Five years, Corey, *five years*, it's going to take you five years to get over this."
>
> I said, "Thank you. Thank you for putting a time limit on it, I can deal with that." When she said five years, everything

was suddenly better. I had been in therapy for a while, but it took Martha to say that for me to snap out of it.

As always, Martha moved on. Friends and family, though, would sometimes see the sadness she carried around about losing her first love.

Eva Scrivo, who was brought in as Martha's hip young hairstylist and makeup artist, remembers a moment only a few years ago in the kitchen at Turkey Hill when Martha was rummaging through papers. She came across some old letters. "Martha saves everything, everything is precious to her—mementos and pictures," says Eva. "She pulled out a letter her husband had written to her when they were first married. She read me the letter out loud and I could see the tears in her eyes. I felt so much the love that she had once had for somebody."

Whatever heartbreak Martha endured, she poured the energy into her work. When her magazine, *Martha Stewart Living*, debuted in 1991, Martha was back to herself—sharp minded and sharp witted. John explains:

> She was all about having fun with what we were doing. We had such a good time. I remember once at Thanksgiving time, I was doing a mirror and the frame was made out of pecans. I got a fifty-pound bag of nuts and I came up in the elevator with the bag. Martha got on the elevator and looked at me and said, "What are you doing with all of these nuts?" I told her I was making a mirror and she said, "Well, why did you have to go buy nuts? We have plenty of nuts working *here*."

Her mind was very quick, and either she liked your idea or she didn't. It saved a lot of time, and Martha was always short on time. Her comments weren't just black or white; she would suggest modifications. But most of the time she loved everything we did, which was really great. Martha would have meetings with us and they were always extremely productive. She would ask us countless questions and was thorough in every respect. If she scolded us, she wasn't trying to humiliate us or trying to make us cower. She assumed we were as strong as she was and that we could take it. She just wanted to get our attention, and that she did.

She was approachable, too. Talking to Martha wasn't like talking to a movie star—it was more like talking to your aunt or talking to a friend. But it was also talking to someone who had done all of the projects herself at one time or another, and who knew exactly what it entailed. Martha was always questioning things—she was always challenging us to come up with new and better ideas. It kept me on top of my game.

She was funny too. I'd be sitting there eating M&M's and she'd walk up and hold her hand out. I thought Martha was very cool. She was always there to guide and cheer us on. She even insisted on eating lunch with us. Having lunch together was important to her.

The caterers who provided lunch for the staff would try to outdo themselves each day, serving succulent prime rib one day and sirloin steaks in heavy French sauces made of butter, cream, and egg yolks the next. I think they were bringing out all this rich food because they were trying to impress her because this was a person you wanted to try to impress.

After a few months of high-calorie feasts, Martha pulled aside one of her staff and said, "You know, you've got to tell them to stop this. Just because I am Martha Stewart doesn't mean I want to die of high cholesterol!"

Not long after, Martha had a gym installed. It was open for everyone to use—and she wanted us to use it. She wanted all of us to be fit and healthy. What she preached in the magazine she conveyed to us and followed in her own life.

With her magazine, Martha wanted to take everything she knew and everything she learned and spread it to as many people as she could. She feels it is her mission in life to make the world a more beautiful place.

"Everyone always asks me, 'What's it like to have Martha as a sister? Did you know she'd be famous?'" says her brother George. "The expectation that she would actually be famous never really approached my conscious level of thinking. I always thought she'll be what she will be and if she gets famous, great. But the quest to perfection can lead to insanity—I drive myself crazy trying to make things be a certain way. It eats at you, and if you've got fifty things going on all at once that all have to be perfect, you can go over the edge really easily."

George would listen in on the frenzied powwows Martha would have in her kitchen with the magazine editorial team as they discussed new ideas for feature stories. "Someone brought up a topic. Martha said, '*Oh, I know*, if you go up to 84th Street to this little store and talk to Jacob, and tell him what you want—but don't let him show you anything in the front, make him take you to the back room and you'll find some really nice stuff that will go with some other stuff that you'll find down in the East Village in another little shop—and put all of that stuff together with some stuff from my basement and we'll get a really great article!' I listened in and thought, Huh? In New York City there was this tiny room in the back of a little store where Martha could go and grab things—who could remember all that stuff? But she could categorize everything in her mind, from shop to shop, from article to article."

When Martha's TV show *Martha Stewart Living* debuted in 1993, it was a whole new forum for her to create perfection. The show was shot on Martha's own turf—her house at Turkey Hill.

One of her former assistants, Lisa Wagner, remembers early on in the show when the crew attempted to bring camera cables and other equipment across the yard. "Martha started yelling, 'They are walking all over the moss!' We had to build a platform. And in the house, it was always, '*Take your shoes off!*'"

I remember from the days when my wife, Leslie, worked in TV commercials that it was a known fact that the camera crew will often trash your house within seconds of their arrival.

In the afternoons, Martha's dogs would run through the kitchen and all over the set. Invariably, right in the middle of a shoot, they'd need to eat. "Oops, the dogs have to be fed!" Martha would say, and someone would peel a boiled egg and crumble it into the dog food bowl so they'd quiet down.

John remembers when a friend of his was hired to faux-paint the kitchen floor of Martha's TV studio to resemble her wood-grained floor at Turkey Hill. When the work was done, Martha inspected the job. "She said, as only she could, 'Oh, this doesn't look exactly like the other floor,' and my friend happily redid the whole thing because she knew that if it had Martha's seal of approval it really meant something. This particular level of craftsmanship, and the drive needed to execute it, is hard for most people to understand."

Eva explains Martha's sensitivity to her surroundings: "Martha is like an artist—she creates beautiful things, she fixes things, and she knows how to create a beautiful world. How can you not have sensitivity? She's hypersensitive; she is so aware of everything going on. She feels things very deeply."

On her first day at Martha's, Eva not only took off her shoes, she wiped her feet on a towel. They got to work in Martha's pristine bathroom when they heard what sounded like a bulldozer in the front yard. Martha glanced out the window to see a procession of trucks barreling onto her beautifully raked stone driveway.

"Martha looked at me sweetly and said, 'Excuse me, dearie,' and then opened the window and poked her head out and yelled, '*Get the hell off my driveway!*'" Eva recalls with a laugh. "Everybody looked up, and I thought to myself, God, she is right. These trucks are ruining all of this beautiful stonework! She closed the window and said, 'Okay, back to work.' It was so funny. It really broke the ice because I saw her be a real person."

Eva still works for Martha after a decade of traveling around the world with her. Eva thinks that Martha is the ultimate trouper. Her favorite example is a TV shoot they did on Hogg's Island, a small island off the coast of San Francisco. For the show, Martha wanted to do a segment about the local fishermen who harvest oysters using big vats. They were to show the audience how to catch oysters, shuck them, and cook them on the barbecue.

The day of the shoot was beautiful — dazzling skies and crisp, cool air. As the crew set up the cameras on shore, Martha donned a pair of waterproof hip boots and hopped on board with the men to go oyster hunting. Eva recalls, "When she came back, her hair was really matted and there was dirt and sand all over her face, but she looked beautiful. She walked toward me and stepped on a wire that was separated from what it was plugged into. Unbeknownst to us, she had half an inch of water in her boots and she was shocked. The shock threw her back five feet and she fell on her back. We all rushed to her and picked her up, and she said, 'I'm fine, I'm fine, don't worry.'"

They started shooting immediately after. About five minutes into it Martha started scratching her foot. She kept reaching down to scratch and finally took her boot off. "We all saw what looked like a large red hole in her foot. And she said, 'Oh my God, is there an insect around here? Something bit me. Is this a snake bite?'"

Martha insisted on finishing the segment because the sun was about to set, and if they stopped it would have ruined a hundred-thousand-dollar shoot day. An hour later, the crew rushed her to the hospital, where a doctor examined her foot and told her that the red hole was actually an exit wound: a bolt of electricity had gone up the left side of her body, bypassed her heart, and left via the right side of her body through her right foot.

"Now if this wasn't a test of strength," says Eva, "of how strong this woman is and what a professional she is!"

But the day wasn't over yet. They had one more shoot to do before sundown. Their next pit stop was a nearby bakery that made the best cinnamon rolls in town. "Martha showed up on crutches and she couldn't put any weight on the right side of her body," says Eva. "When she was about to film, she asked me to take the crutches away and she did the entire segment standing on one leg."

More than being a trouper, Martha, Eva believes, is a champion of the entrepreneur in the way she has helped other women get ahead. Two weeks before President Bill Clinton moved out of the White House for the new administration to move in, Martha and Eva attended a party in the grand hallway. As Martha chatted with Hillary Clinton, she pulled Eva into the conversation. Eva says, "She told Hillary, 'I want you to meet Eva. She is the best hair and makeup artist. You *have* to have her do your hair. She has a great salon in New York and you must go there.' Meanwhile there were thirty people all standing around holding their hands looking at these two ladies, never daring to interrupt, waiting for them to get done. It was so funny; I was so embarrassed I just wanted to hide. She was trying to get Hillary Clinton as my client!"

The day Evelyn Lauder came to Turkey Hill to be interviewed on Martha's show, Martha made sure Eva would be at the house. "She said, 'She is really big, Evelyn Lauder. We have to talk to her about you doing her hair and makeup, and then I'll introduce you. It was like she was plotting with me!"

Eva attributes her success to Martha. "It's all because of Martha. I know Martha was put into my life for a reason. I came from very humble beginnings—my parents probably would have been thrilled if I made really good money waitressing and married a really nice guy—they would have thought I had done really well in my life. Meeting Martha woke me up, and I realized, oh my God, life can be this way, I can have so many things. She raised the bar for me and made me think big."

Corey ended up coming back to work for Martha—(as many have over the years). He says working on the TV show was great fun, especially when Martha was in one of her mischievous moods.

Remember when the Miracle Bra came out? Victoria's Secret was doing an advertising blitz and the bra was getting an extraordinary amount of press. One day around that time we were shooting in the Easter Field, a piece of land adjacent to Martha's Turkey Hill property that has two splendid areas of cutting flowers.

Martha was waiting for the shot to be set up. I remember she was in a particularly good mood that morning. The production crew had a huge piece of equipment in the field, a platform lift that could ascend and descend three stories allowing for fantastic camera angles and an incredible view of Long Island Sound. The guys who operated the lift were taking me up and down, goofing around, and I was getting dizzier and dizzier.

Martha was sitting below in her folding chair talking on her cell phone, which at that time was brand-new technology. When I finally got down from the height of the lift, I couldn't stop babbling about the superpowers of the Miracle Bra, but to the wrong audience—the female producer on the set. I went on and on how the bra didn't just lift, separate, and enhance, but it could transform mousy librarians into femmes fatales. The producer went stone-faced.

Martha overheard my banter and became my willing accomplice. She announced to the whole crew that she herself was wearing a Miracle Bra and then asked the producer if she was wearing one, too. She continued asking other people, then she suggested that maybe she could get Victoria's Secret to sponsor the show because yes, indeed, the bra did what it advertised—it had completely changed her life!

Corey remembers watching footage one day of Martha attempting to record sound bites for her show. It is sure to be used someday on some TV bloopers special. "Martha was saying; 'This is Martha Stewart for WKPZ in Des Moines. Be sure to watch Martha Stewart Living at six A.M. today. Six A.M.! *Damn* it! *Bleep*! *Bleep*! Who the *bleep* is going to *bleeping* watch at six A.M.?' Then a voice said, 'Cut!' and she would have to say these sound bites over and over again, cursing in between. It was so funny and a little bizarre at the same time."

With both the magazine and her TV show to contend with— and the business aspects of her huge licensing deal with

Kmart—the work schedule was grueling, even for Martha, who thrived on long hours.

The TV producers would try to get all the cooking segments out of the way first because they were the most difficult. Then they'd tackle crafts and "good things" and smaller projects. Some days, Martha would have to go on location and visit stores in Manhattan or an incredible garden in some other country. They all tried to keep sane at the insane pace with a dose of humor, says John. "I remember one time a plumber was fixing Martha's shower," he recalls. "She had a full working bathroom, because after she would finish on the set she wanted to shower off all the heavy makeup; also the lights were incredibly warm. The plumber left his tools all over the floor, and it was a bit of a mess. He went out to the truck to get a part or something. Martha went into the bathroom and came out roaring at the top of her lungs, '*Who made this mess?*' I stood there, speechless. I didn't know what to do. Then she just burst out laughing when she saw that she had scared me to death."

Martha and Lexi share an off-kilter sense of humor that is sometimes misunderstood by people who don't know them.

"Martha is human," John says. "She had times when things were super-stressful. She was running three different companies: Martha by Mail, Martha Stewart Everyday for Kmart, and Martha Stewart Living. The dogs were outside fighting with each other, and she was inside trying to hold it together. Her mother was there talking away about something, and the secretary was saying, 'You have a phone call on line six,' and all six lines were blinking. It was a lot for any one person to handle, man or woman. Martha was always doing fifteen things at once and doing them perfectly."

"If she wasn't feeling attractive that day, or if she was unhappy, things always got misdirected at the people closest to her," says Eva, "because in a family, that's what happens. But with Martha, there was quick recovery time. She would say, 'Oh, it's not you . . . I'm just feeling x, y, and z today.' She would always make it up to you."

The unspoken rule on set was that you had to stay away from Martha toward the end of a shoot day—if you had something to ask her, do it in the morning. As one former colleague says, if you approached late in the day, "it was almost guaranteed she was going to throw a fit."

"Humor was our only survival technique," says the colleague. "We'd all be running around doing our stuff and the studio monitor would be on and you'd be thinking, oh my gosh, she's going off again. It was like a soap opera. We would all get together and didn't know whether to laugh or cry about it. The laughter was like a weird defense mechanism."

Another former colleague puts it like this: "Martha can be either completely wonderful and charming or the biggest bitch in the entire world—you either get one or the other."

"We cared—we tried to protect her from herself so many times," one employee told me. "It's like being in the Oval Office with the president of the United States going off on a temper tantrum and threatening to blow up the world. You're just there to support her and put out fires. Martha puts so much pressure on herself and she doesn't have to. But that's her."

Lexi doesn't understand what all the fuss is about when she hears people complaining that her mother micromanages:

> So what if it's true? How are you going to start a business like that and not be controlling? She should walk into the office and say, "Do whatever you want, I don't care"? Yeah, that would make a good magazine or TV show. You know what, "Here's some toys, go play with them and we'll take pictures."
>
> Find me another human being who runs a large company who isn't controlling. How could she not be? She'd be an idiot if she weren't. She wouldn't be who she is and this all wouldn't matter. I also find it quite sexist.
>
> No one was ever chained down and made to stay. The press never goes to the people who have been with her for twenty years and asks them what it's like to work with her. Those are the people who stuck it out, had something to offer, and helped her build a great brand.

Martha's intentions were good. Her attempts to make the show perfect were for her fans. She didn't want to talk down to her viewers, and she didn't want to show them something that wasn't done right; that wasn't done the way *she herself* would do it. Lisa observes:

> People would say to her, "Martha, it's television, you can't see if the berries are slightly overripe or the knife is not sharp; no one will know it's not a perfectly ripe apricot." But *she* would know. It drove the TV people crazy. The

other thing that drove them crazy was that whatever she was doing had to be completed. In television, you try to be as efficient as possible.

You didn't need to roll out all the rest of those tart shells! We saw it, we know how to do it, someone else can do it later. No—she wanted the tart shells all rolled out perfectly so they would all be done. What she made had to be delicious, even though the TV audience couldn't tell if it tasted good. TV producers would come in to the set from the outside and say, "*Are you nuts!* She rolls out two and we go on to the next step!"

It was funny, because you just knew that all Martha wanted was that finished tart shell for some lunch tomorrow. Why waste it? "I am having so and so for dinner tomorrow, and I want this for that, so we're finishing it. No, we can't move on to the next set."

It was tough to get her to short-cut anything. We had directors come in and say, "You can't spend this amount of time taping something; it's going to be cut down to five minutes anyway. You have to short-cut it," but she felt like she was cheating the audience if she did. She'd say, "I'm not dumbing it down." Martha had such respect for her audience. She was going to give them what they wanted and she was going to show them every step.

Sometimes she was way too sophisticated. We balanced that with things that were simple, but then occasionally we'd have to show them how to make supercomplicated puff pastries and it would take half a day.

The end result was a gorgeous thing. There was nothing

else on television that looked like that, that had that amount of care and time and money put into it. It was just beautiful, such a luxury. But it was also very tough. We would put it up and take it down; the show was in her house and things broke and it was difficult.

When we became a daily show, it was a *huge* undertaking, and then we had to do an hour because the stations needed to fill that block. That was a huge challenge, and we struggled to retain every bit of quality. No one wanted to give up, especially Martha.

Martha kept up her hectic pace by day, and at night attempted to wind down. John says, "She told me that at three in the morning she would get solace from ironing her linen or damask dinner napkins while watching TV. That was her peace. When she was especially exhausted, once in a while she'd be caught taking an unintentional catnap during a meeting with Kmart executives."

Well, didn't she deserve a nap?

7

The Going Gets Tough

There's a side of her that a lot of people don't see
and don't know about—how much fun and funny
she is and how down-to-earth she can be.

—LISA WAGNER

In between all the hard work, Martha and her employees managed to slip in some fun and let their hair down. Eva Scrivo recalls the day Martha called her up in the Hamptons and said, "Get ready. I've got the dogs with me and we're going out for dinner!"

She picked me up and we went to Nick and Toni's. She wanted to go to the bar because it was more fun than sitting at a table in the dining room. We ordered appetizers and because she was with this young girl — me — we ordered cosmos. We ended up getting really toasted. A writer for a Hamptons magazine came up and acted like her best friend. She didn't remember who he was, you know — this happens all the time. We also didn't know if he was hitting on me or her. The guy took out some tobacco and rolled a cigarette at the bar and asked Martha if she wanted one.

Now this is a woman who is against smoking and throws anyone off her property if they're smoking. But we were really buzzed. So he gave us two for the road, and it looked like he was giving us a joint. Martha and I left in her Suburban after ditching the cigarettes in the parking lot. We drove home and she was just so funny. Deep down in her heart, she is just like me or you—she wants to connect and have fun and have a buzz and gossip.

Martha can get starstruck as well. After introducing Eva to Hillary Clinton at the White House, she convinced Clinton to hire Eva to work her magic on the new senator for a party that night. So Eva went up to Hillary's ultra-private apartment. Eva recalls, "When we got into the airplane to go home, Martha turned into a total girl and said, 'Oh my God, what was it like up there?' Because nobody goes up to the private apartment. It was really cute, because she wanted to know what it was like. She asked, 'So, how was it decorated? Did she have her own private vanity room?' Martha loves to just be a girl."

If Martha's team was scheduled to do a shoot somewhere interesting, Martha would make sure they took in some culture. "Martha would get the curator of the museum of wherever we were to open at seven in the morning for us before a shoot because she wanted us to see something wonderful and inspiring," says Eva. "Even though it was extra work, she would make time for these things and she would invite people to come with her. If we were somewhere where there was a nature habitat, she would get up at five and take a walk through a garden or through a portion of a rainforest, just so life wasn't always about work. Work was play, too."

For a shoot one day on a windy bluff in Rhode Island, Martha was teaching her viewers how to do a crab boil. She beckoned to her staff to get into the shot. "She said, 'Come on, be in this with me," says Lisa Wagner. "We had been up since dawn and we looked a wreck and had been working all day, but she wanted us to be on camera with her because it would be more fun for her. It *was* fun. We found some blue workshirts out of wardrobe and we did the crab boil with her. It really made her happy to have someone doing it with her."

Judy Morris began working as Martha's assistant after an hour-long interview during which, Judy says, they "just chatted and got to know each other. Martha knew that if you were a good person and she liked you and connected with you, the rest would fall into place." Until she found an apartment in Westport, Judy lived in Martha's barn, because "being her assistant involved every-thing and you needed to be close to her twenty-four hours a day. So every morning, the chickens would wake me up. I became part of the family." And Martha's traveling eating partner.

"Once a month I would set up lectures for anywhere from two to five thousand women and we would put together a slide show. That was always fun, because I had a chance to travel with Martha. Until you travel with Martha, you don't fully know Martha. She is amazing to travel with because you have to have whatever that city is best known for—you have to eat the very best thing, you have to drink the very best thing, you have to visit the very best places. Somehow she gets it done in a matter of twenty-four hours—you've seen the city and you've tasted the city."

On one lecture trip to New Orleans, Martha brought along

some editors from the magazine to search the city for new ideas and look for their best antiques. Eight of them arrived on a private plane. Judy explains:

> We divided and conquered—four of us went to the lecture, the other four had fun antiquing. After the lecture we all met up and went to some little café to have the best fried dough at the most famous place to have it. And then we had to go have a Cajun martini with the edge rimmed in Cajun spices. Then we had to figure out the best, best, *best* place to eat in New Orleans, so we were all on our different cell phones, calling contacts, doing whatever we needed to do. "No, let's go here, no, let's go there, no, let's go there. Okay, you go in this car and call us with what's good and we'll go in this car—"
>
> Somehow I ended up by myself in the stretch limo and the other seven people ended up crammed into the little town car. I wound up in the worst possible neighborhood outside New Orleans in a shack that apparently served the best possible food in New Orleans. My limo was literally as long as this little restaurant. I was all by myself and I got out of the huge limo and looked for Martha. And of course she wasn't there. But somehow we all connected and we ended up having a delicious meal.
>
> Eating with Martha is always the most amazing experience, because you sit back and she orders the best things and then the chef comes out. It's just a real treat.

Dinner with Martha is also funny. "She cracks me up," says Judy. "She always calls a place a 'joint.' She'll say, 'What's going on around this joint?' She's serious, but you just have to crack up laughing."

One year Martha was partnered with the rapper Busta Rhymes to give an award at the MTV Video Music Awards. "She kept asking us, 'Who is Busta Rhymes? *Who is this Busta Rhymes?*' She had no clue. Then they struck up such a rapport that she invited him to our Christmas party at the studio! Here's this major rapper and America's favorite homemaker—together. They were such a funny couple."

"Men were so attracted to her," says John Hanson. "She was so sexy. After I finished working at *Martha,* I went off and did interior decorating and image consulting in the city, and I worked for a man who owned a very powerful hedge fund. He was a closet Martha Stewart watcher. He wouldn't even admit it in front of his wife, but he admitted it to me."

Even Corey Tippin admits to having a crush on Martha. "I wrote her letters," he says, "in purple ink, and I would seal and stamp them with a wax seal. It was sweet—playful and flirtatious, fun and childish. I was Martha's merry prankster, and most of the time she was amused by it."

Martha appreciates whatever unique talent or creation a person can offer, no matter who you are. On one trip to San Francisco, Lisa remembers, the plane had to stop and refuel in Nebraska:

Martha made sure that we called ahead, because Nebraska, she said, had the "best bacon and egg sandwiches ever." We landed, refueled, and we had the best bacon and egg sandwiches we've ever had made by some local farmer. That's what it was like to be with her. It didn't have to be the finest place, but just who makes the best local food in that town. So many people think, Oh, Martha's coming, we need to put out the fancy tablecloth. But that isn't what she really wants.

Once, we were driving along the roads in Puerto Rico and we saw flames—they were cooking pigs on the side of the road! We had to stop, and Martha asked them, "How do you do it? What is that? Give me ten of them!"

"She loves to connect with people," says Eva. "She loves when she can really talk to somebody and laugh and have a good time even if she has nothing in common with them. But say they do something beautiful, like all the artisans she meets traveling around the country—the women who made salmon over an open fire on a cedar plank, for example, she really connected with those women. They had nothing in common, but Martha thinks whatever anyone does is important."

Later, when she was on tour for some of the Kmart stores in the Midwest, Martha delighted in meeting her fans. One night after she had finished a housewares presentation, she overheard some of the women chatting about where they were going to go for dinner. "Find out where they're going," she whispered to her assistant. And to the surprise of those suburban ladies, Martha not only showed up at their restaurant, she joined them for dinner.

"She genuinely enjoyed their company," says Eva. "Martha was always doing things like this. It helped her keep in touch with the interests of other ordinary women. Remember, ordinary to Martha is extraordinary."

"There were great times like at two in the morning when we'd be together making flower arrangements in our pajamas," says Judy. "Yes, there's the side of Martha that you see in a meeting or a quick encounter in a restaurant and people think they know the real Martha. But it's when you are with her in her down-time—she obviously works seven days a week, twenty-four hours a day, so she has no real downtime—but when you are with her traveling or at her home at two A.M., that's when you start to see a whole other side to her."

Judy remembers a day when she was frantically trying to get to the airport for a business trip they were to take. Judy was late, and Martha, who is always punctual, was waiting in the plane on the tarmac:

> I got on the plane, and Martha could not have been sweeter. She said, "Okay, you are going to sit right here. I brought some homemade applesauce that I froze so now it's not so slushy and I'm putting it over the best pure organic yogurt." She likes to be the stewardess—she serves everybody, so even flying with her is fun.
>
> She took me to Japan for the Olympics—she was doing *CBS This Morning,* and they wanted her to go to the Olympics for the week and be a correspondent. I went in advance to check things out and scout some of the locations. I remember feeling completely alone. I'd never been to Japan before in my life—the language was so different, the culture so different. The people from CBS made me feel even more alone because they were so busy doing their thing, and I was just a Martha Stewart person—in the way.

The day Martha showed up, I remember the feeling that it was like seeing my mom, I was so excited to see her. As soon as she arrived, the fun started happening. We started going out to dinner; I was eating green-tea ice cream and trying all the best sakes and the great sushi. She wanted me to see the country and experience the culture, not just work.

We went up to the mountains, we saw the monkeys, and we just did *everything*. When we were on the bus, a rickety old bus, driving back to the airport, I was half asleep and I kind of woke up in a fog—and I called her Mom. That's how nurturing she was during that trip. I felt very comfortable with her. I have been with a couple of people who have worked with her that have accidentally called her Mom, because that's what she was to everyone in a way— she really took care of us.

Judy started working for Martha when she was twenty-three. She says:

She went through all my dating years with me, my engagement, my wedding, and then when I was pregnant she was really sweet with it. I went into her office one day to show her the ultrasound picture of the baby. I said, "Here you go," and it took her a second, then she was so thrilled and happy.

They put me on television nine months pregnant, which is always a treat, in the middle of the summer at the end of July. I did a segment on packing a maternity bag. Martha packed the bag and helped me build my changing table. We got all organized, and they bought everything—you know, all the diapers, the onesies, the burp clothes, all the ear syringe things—I mean they gave me *everything*. Martha told me what each thing was for. That was a really nice segment.

Then it was the weekend of Martha's birthday. My water broke that Friday night. Martha's birthday was on Saturday and my mother's birthday was on Sunday! I called Martha. She said, "Oh great! Have the baby on my birthday!" The baby came on my mother's birthday. I called Martha from the hospital and she was just thrilled. At the same time, I was watching television and I swear to God the segment aired with me packing my bag to go to the hospital. So there I was, holding my baby in my arms for the first time and all the nurses were coming around and saying, "Oh my God, there you are on television!"

I was home for maybe a day or two, and I got a call from my dear friend Carolyn Kelly-Wallach, one of Martha's assistants, saying, "Martha and I are on our way, we'll be there in ten minutes," then click; she hung up. I flew into a frenzy, trying to clean up the house as best I could, and then I thought, you know what, Martha doesn't care, I'm not going to be like everyone else freaking out because Martha Stewart is coming over. It is what it is.

Martha walked in and grabbed the baby and sat down. It was the best visit. She brought fresh eggs and fresh tomatoes from her garden. Carolyn had brought me a beautiful sling for the baby but Martha was upset that it smelled a little too perfumy, so she insisted on hand washing it. She was at the sink washing out this thing, and she said, "Okay, where are your lines?"

"Lines? What are you talking about, lines?"

"You know, the laundry line outside to hang this up!"

"Uh, Martha, I don't have a laundry line."

Then she noticed that the baby's feet were purple. I said, "I don't know why but they do get purple, but I read in a book that the circulation on babies is a little bit messed up and they do some funky things."

She said, "No, Judy, I think the diaper is too tight." She took off the diaper, then all of a sudden, *boop*, these little purple feet turned a perfect pink.

I said, "You better not tell anybody this story—you better not go back to the studio and tell everybody." Sure enough, I saw them on TV doing a montage for the show opening. They were all sitting around a table having dinner talking about the purple feet on the baby and the diaper being too tight.

Besides Martha's need for perfection, many close friends say that if they were to identify what causes Martha to lash out, it would be that she has trouble connecting with people on a very intimate level. She can have fun with you and can discuss all sorts of topics, but she doesn't share with you her biggest disappointments and fears. "She can't, it's just not part of her makeup," says one former colleague. "She would be the first to admit to this and be sad about it. She is not able to let her hair down the way girlfriends do with one another. She can't deal with emotions the way most people do. And yet you can sometimes feel how desperately she wants to have someone to talk to."

This makes it all the more difficult for her to let people out of her life, no matter how much they may have disappointed her. Eva says:

> She feels such loyalty to people, because she was raised to be so responsible for everyone, to take care of everyone. When people have not done a good job, or have acted inappropriately, if they touched her heart she kept them on and kept them in her life. She worried about how they would support their family. She would say, "Oh, they have children, and they've been with me a long time," and she would refuse to fire them.
>
> I told her time and time again, "You should get rid of him," but she felt their job was not merely judged on their performance but how long they have been with her. Loyalty is a big thing for her, and it has gotten her into trouble. She's too kind in a lot of circumstances. And then she'll get kind of mad at herself that these people are still in her life.

In 1997 Lexi fell in love with a young lawyer and decided to get married. Foreseeing a possible frenzy with the press, she and her fiancé planned to elope. She explains, "To be nice to my mother, we did not. She would have been sad if I had done that. I had to include her in my wedding. She's my mother!"

The wedding was so low-key and un-Martha-like, though, that the press called it a snub by Lexi. Lexi denies that adamantly:

> You can fantasize all you want; it didn't have anything to do with my mother. And don't believe the rumors that she was

upset that it wasn't a big wedding, because she wasn't. This gets back to the same old cliché. This is exactly what her critics want you to believe, that she is telling me or you what to do or how to live your life. She merely puts examples out there for people to pick which ones they want to follow.

If you want to have a giant wedding, here are some of her ideas. If you want to have a little wedding where you make your own wedding cake, that's wonderful too and here are the instructions for a cake. If you just want to go to a restaurant and have lunch, that's okay, too. She's just not going to put that one in the magazine.

The new mother-in-law kindly offered her services for the postwedding week. Lexi took her up on that offer. "Our honeymoon was even a nonevent," Lexi says, laughing. "She offered us her home in Maine and we accepted. That was perfect for me. Being alone, hidden, staying in a big house and walking through unbelievable gardens made for a wonderful honeymoon. When the honeymoon was over, I told my mom that the house needed to be remodeled. When she thought about it, she agreed. Now who's control-freaking whom?"

During this time, Martha kept up with the rest of the family, hiring her sister Laura as producer for her syndicated radio show. The show was on five days a week on over 270 stations, with an audience of one and a half million listeners. Laura says:

It really fit into my lifestyle. It was a nice thing for me because I could stay at home and be there for my family and work part time. The theme of the radio show was "You can learn something new every day," and I was indeed learning a whole lot of new things every day. Because I know Martha so well and I knew that every week would have to be a balance of topics, every week there were five interesting things that I wrote about and that she would read. Every two weeks we would record.

It was a highlight for her, because it was early in the morning before her TV day and she would sit and read ten radio shows in the sound room. She always said it was one of her favorite parts of the business because it was an informal learning time. Plus it was a great show!

In the late nineties, as Martha's career reached stellar proportions, she was a regular on the late-night talk-show circuit and showed a flair for pleasing her hosts and the audience. Judy says:

Martha would ignore all their stupid little jokes and they would melt. For one appearance on the Conan O'Brien show that was to air Thanksgiving week, we were going to make a turkey. So we went to Martha and said, "How do you want to make it funny, how do you want to put a spin on this?" She said, "Why don't we bring all my turkeys from Turkey Hill?" And I looked at her like she was crazy, but I said okay.

I loaded up her old Suburban and drove down Park Avenue with about fifteen turkeys clucking in the back, and I thought, What the hell have I gotten myself into? This woman is crazy! Then we unloaded these fifteen turkeys at

Rockefeller Center to go up to the Conan studios. It was hysterical. We had a big pen out and all the turkeys were walking around. Conan loved it. He fell in love with her—as everybody does. That's the spontaneity you learn from being around Martha for more than ten years—you can do it, you can make it happen, don't worry about it, it's not a big deal.

Before shooting an appearance on David Letterman's show, "I stood backstage preparing the prop food projects that Dave and Martha would joke about as I listened to Dave's warm-up," says Corey Tippin. "He was rousing the audience up with his sarcasm about Martha. I felt tremendous sympathy for her that night. Letterman continued to be so nasty that I was almost in tears. Martha endured it all. She always focused on the big picture and let the petty frat-boy humor roll off her. She may have had a sense of humor about David Letterman, but I lost mine."

One Halloween night, after Martha had finished shooting a Halloween show using hundreds of pieces of candy as decoration, she called Necy Fernandez to pack up the candy and take it home. Necy recalls:

> Martha said, "Necy, find my witch hat for me." She had a big hat and a black dress. "I don't have time to stop and do it, because I'm coming home late. Can you bag the candies and just decorate a little bit?" So I decorated the entrance of the house. She usually never opened up the little gate, but that night she opened up the little gate. And she dressed up in her witch costume.

The next day I came back and Martha said, "Necy, all that candy is gone! I know there was tons of candy." So a few days went by and it was in the news: "Talk about how mean Martha Stewart was—when the people got there she closed the gate!" I was so upset. We had given out all the candy and had to close the gates. People lied just to say mean things.

When it comes to the media, Lexi feels protective about her mother:

My mother never tried to protect me from the media. I don't think I needed protection. I didn't want to be in the media spotlight and I wasn't. She's the one who could have used some protection. I just don't understand why people can be so pathetic. They don't even know my mother and they write mean things to sell papers and get ratings. I can't believe everyone wants bad news. It's sick!

People don't get in my face about my mother. Maybe they're afraid of getting confronted. I don't know. I feel like smacking some of the people that make up these stories. My mother feels like the world has let her down. The press took the messages and lifestyle that she presents and made fun of it. These negative writers are losers and should be making fun of something else, in my opinion. It's only a few that hate her, but they make a lot of noise and have confused a lot of people. Her fans, though, know what she's all about.

Martha could find the media funny as well. Corey recalls:

There was a time that we did a very early morning segment for the *Today* show live from Martha's vegetable garden. It featured soil preparation and it involved her using that rather barbaric-looking garden tool known as the Garden Weasel. Remember the ads on TV? It was a spiky medieval-looking object attached to a rake handle. By pushing and pulling the device, it would break up clumps in the soil before planting.

There is a shot called the teaser that airs right before a show goes to commercial; teasers introduce the segments that are going to air over the next fifteen minutes. This teaser said something like, "Stay tuned for Martha Stewart, live from her garden in Westport." Coming up next after the teaser was a movie review. That day the review was of *Serial Mom*, a John Waters film. After the review, Martha's segment was to air.

The review showed a clip from *Serial Mom* that was particularly violent, in which the serial killer mom, played by Kathleen Turner, clubs a neighbor to death with a leg of lamb. It was hilarious! Immediately afterward, they interviewed John Waters, and he said, "The lead character was inspired by Martha Stewart."

Then the show cut to Martha's teaser, where she was wielding the Weasel, then it cut to commercial. I gasped and turned to Martha, who was busily working, to explain to her that she had just been set up. At first her face registered horror. But a second later, she raised up her Weasel and deadpanned, "Oh my God, it's finally happened. I've become a caricature of myself!"

In 1999 when Martha went on national TV and rang the opening bell at the New York Stock Exchange, handing out brioches and fresh-squeezed orange juice, some people heard it as the death knell for her career. After all, in this country, you can be a woman and a great success, but if you become a billionaire and tread into the testosterone-driven waters of Wall Street, you just might engender the wrath of the powers that be.

"It's an interesting point to touch upon," says one of Martha's friends. "We are socialized as men and women in this culture and it is very uncomfortable for us to see women in a position of power. Martha is a kind of androgynous person—I never really see her as terribly feminine or terribly masculine. When a woman is in a powerful situation, that can make us uncomfortable. I think that it's kind of terrifying for us to see a woman not only not act like a woman, but act neither masculine nor feminine—simply assertive."

Another by-product of fame that was especially distressing for Martha—a woman who needed to connect but didn't always know how, who needed to know what was going on in all areas at all times—was the isolation celebrity brought.

"Martha always wanted to be treated normally," says Eva. "People were afraid of that position of power she had. They wouldn't say hello to her at her own company. She didn't know who the interns were—there would be assistants coming and going and they wouldn't even say hello to her or 'Thank you for allowing me to be part of this company. I've learned so much.' They were afraid of her. Being ostracized like that in her own world—*a world she had created*—was very frustrating to her."

The extent of her frustration was evident only in rare

moments. Her friend Corey is still haunted by an unguarded moment he witnessed during a shoot in her backyard one day:

It was a particularly horrible day and there was a guest staying at her house—somebody famous. Martha came out in the morning and was ranting to the guys. The roses this, the trees that. Everything was bothering her, and I said, "Martha, stop it." Really. I don't know where it came from but I said again, "*Stop it.*" She was humiliating herself and I didn't want this to happen.

So she did. She stopped and she went and got her makeup on. One of the producers said, "This is a very tense day and we want everything to go perfectly and we don't want any mistakes so I want you to have everything and more that Martha needs for this show, and if anything's missing there is going to be a *big problem*. I want you to be totally prepared today."

For the shot, Corey had assembled all the gardening tools needed for that particular segment and placed them all in a wheelbarrow.

But when we started filming the segment and one of the assistants asked for something while Martha was on the set, it wasn't there. Martha tightly said, "I'll find it," and started fumbling around in the wheelbarrow. The set was dead silent. You could feel that something was terribly, terribly wrong. It wasn't just that something was missing—it was something more than that.

I followed Martha to the old garden shed. She was moving around, searching, and saying over and over, "I want everybody to go away. I want this to stop. I want to be alone. Just everyone leave me alone."

"Martha," I said softly.

"What!"

"You know we all love you."

And she stopped. She turned around, looked at me, and started crying. I hugged her and looked into her eyes. Her mascara had run from the tears.

"You understand?" she asked. "*You understand?*"

And I simply said, "Yes, I do understand."

I was completely amazed that this was happening. Eventually we broke away. Martha said with determination, "I'll find that thing, Corey. How come you didn't have it?"

Just like that, she totally turned it around and was back in typical character. But we both knew; we had an understanding. Martha went back out on the set to finish the shoot.

Corey had never told this story to anyone until now. He feels it shows a vulnerability in Martha most never see—and it is time they do.

8

On Trial

She really has a lot of kindness in her.

EVA SCRIVO

A week after Martha was indicted on nine criminal counts from the Securities and Exchange Commission in June 2003, she had a phone chat with her friend and former assistant Lisa Wagner. Both women tried desperately to keep the conversation light, and in an effort to divert Martha's attention from her legal woes, Lisa directed her to a familiar and easy topic: party planning.

"'I have to do a bar mitzvah party for my son. What am I going to do? It has to be different."

"Let's do it in my hay barn up in Bedford!" Martha suggested.

"What? But, oh, God, Martha, do you really think—"

"Don't worry, Lisa," Martha said quickly. "All that doesn't matter. Everything's going to be fine. And anyway, this is what keeps me going, what keeps me *Martha*. This is the kind of stuff we live for, and doing this is what makes me happy."

Martha needed some cheering up, and it wasn't just because of the indictment. All year, throughout the stress of the investigation, she also had to endure the pain of watching her dear friend and colleague Carolyn Kelly-Wallach die from cancer. Carolyn was one of the assistants who was closest to Martha and she was considered a family member. She had worked with Martha from the beginning of Martha's television show and was in charge of Martha's wardrobe. A few weeks earlier, Martha had won an Emmy for her television show, and in her acceptance speech onstage she dedicated the award to Carolyn. The next day, Martha flew back to New York and went to Carolyn's bedside to hand her her producer's Emmy. It was an emotional visit for both of them.

Now, Martha and Lisa got to work clearing out the hay barn, moving the tractors out, and decorating the barn for the party. Martha was trying hard to focus on family and friends, knowing she needed their emotional support now more than ever.

At the party several weeks later, Martha gave a warm and loving speech about Lisa's son, whom she had known since he was four years old. "After she spoke, people at the party came up to me and said, 'God, my impression of her has so changed!'" Lisa recalls. "She was so nice and so sincere. She spoke to everyone at the party, and she was really moved at the whole thing. She couldn't have done a nicer thing."

Martha tried to keep relaxed throughout the summer, working on her garden and socializing. In August, Renny Reynolds bumped into her in a restaurant on Cranberry Island, a remote island off the coast of Maine. "Cranberry isn't more than a few square miles and is in the reeds off the beaten path," says Renny.

"I never thought for a moment I would run into anyone I might know on this island at this particular restaurant."

Renny was with several guests. As they walked in he heard Martha call out to him from her table. "Oh, *Renny!*"

Renny introduced his guests to Martha and they chatted for a few moments, then went to their table to begin their meal. After they finished their meals, Renny went over to say good-bye to Martha. She asked if he'd like to come over and see the house. The "house" was the Ford Mansion, a local historic site that Martha owned. She had located the original garden plans for the house that were created by the famous designer Jen Jenson, but which never had been implemented by the house's original inhabitants.

"Martha somehow got these plans and carried out every detail in them. I was dying to see Martha's gardens. I was beside myself. You can just imagine my guests' delight." The next day, Renny and his guests dropped over for what they thought would be a brief visit:

We toured the house and the grounds and we were entertained with a light lunch. Martha showed us every room. She reveled in the historical implications of the architecture and landscaping. Right down to the linens that came with the estate — it was all big history to her. To implement the gardens, she brought over a well-known gardener from England.

As we were about to leave, I noticed that even the gravel on the driveway was impeccably groomed. I complimented her. "Why Martha, even the gravel is in perfect condition."

"Oh, yes, Renny, we take the gravel up in the fall and put it back in the spring," she told me.

Meanwhile, Martha's family was going through an emotional wringer. "When my sister was indicted it was hard," says Laura. "There were a lot of raw feelings. People were being so mean. At the time, I was very concerned about image and what people might say to my son in school and even people's reactions to me. Now I don't care nearly as much. What's done is done and Martha is obviously Martha and she is going to stand on her feet no matter what happens. I'm proud of Martha's accomplishments, but I can't say I'm proud of what happened. I think that Martha gets herself into trouble sometimes by her actions or what she says."

That winter, during the trial, the code word among Martha's family and closest friends was "canary." This was Martha's new, top-secret e-mail moniker that only a handful of people knew. My first thought was that she picked it to symbolize a canary in a coal mine, based on the tradition of taking canaries into mines to detect hazardous, possibly deadly, conditions ahead. Then, maybe she meant canary diamonds, rare fancy yellow diamonds. Actually, she was making a reference to the canaries she keeps as pets in her aviary at Turkey Hill.

Each day before court, Martha and Alexis would make a very early morning stop at Eva Scrivo's salon in Tribeca to get their hair and makeup done.

"Every morning of the trial, she'd try to act normal with me," says Eva. "She'd want to joke around and laugh, even though these were the most unnormal circumstances."

After three frustrating weeks of reading the newspapers and

watching coverage of the trial on television, I went to the court-house myself. Laura had asked me to come along with her for support.

It was freezing cold that February morning. I picked up Laura at seven A.M. so we could take the train to Manhattan together. During the ride, we sipped coffees and tried to read the *New York Times* but it was no use; we couldn't focus. Our minds were on Martha. We couldn't talk about it, though, for fear that people on the train would overhear us. So we sat, silently, wondering what to expect from the day's testimony.

As we climbed the steps to the federal courthouse, Laura's college-age daughter, Sophie Herbert, ran up to us from her spot behind the rope in the photographer's pit outside. A talented young artist, Sophie was on a secret mission to document her aunt's ordeal for the family archives. Hauling her heavy, classic, twin-reflex camera around her neck, she had somehow managed to embed herself in the photo pool with the rest of the paparazzi, who had no idea she was the niece of Martha Stewart. If any of the photographers made any remarks about her beloved aunt, young Sophie defended her. Sophie says:

Martha has always, *always* been there for my family and me, from the time I was born to the time my father passed away. When I was growing up, she paid for my music lessons and she always encouraged me. Although, when she found out I was applying to art school, she did say, "Don't apply to art school. You won't be able to speak a single sentence when you get out!"

When we were young, she took my brother and me on

all these trips with her—Ecuador, the Galapagos, Egypt, Peru, Brazil, the Amazon—the idea of traveling and exposing a child at a very young age to the Third World to see poverty and suffering was an incredible thing to do. She expanded my horizons. Those trips helped shape my perspective of the world.

Sophie went to art school in Paris in the summer of 2004 and went on a spiritual sojourn through India from 2004 to 2005. "Aunt Martha encouraged it. I worked and made most of my money, but she helped out and I am grateful. The fact that she shares her wealth for people's education is so wonderful."

Laura and I gave Sophie a kiss good-bye and made our way through the metal detectors at the building's entrance. After we passed the inspection, we handed over our cell phones, which the desk clerks put into identical little cubbyholes side by side and then gave us each a ticket stub so we could pick them up at the end of the day.

Inside the courtroom we were led to the left side, the defendants' side of the room. We took seats in the second row, one of the two rows designated for family and close friends.

"Here's Martha," Laura whispered in my ear. I craned my head to see Martha arrive from the back of the room with Alexis, her legal entourage, and a bodyguard. As she passed us, I stood to give her a big hug.

"You look great" was my only remark. Martha was wearing a brown tweed skirt and jacket that was nipped at the waist and slightly ruffled. She stood up tall, squared her shoulders, and tugged the bottom of her jacket straight, as if to smooth out any creases.

"Thank you for coming," she said, then took her place at the defendant's table, giving a smile to Peter Bacanovic, her former stockbroker and codefendant, who was sitting at the next table. She scanned the room with an air of confidence.

Wearing a black Calvin Klein pantsuit, Alexis took a seat in front of me, whipped out the *New York Times* crossword from her black Hermès bag, and started chipping away at it in pen.

All eyes were on Martha. The courtroom was so hushed, I felt as if we were in a church awaiting a sermon. The judge arrived and within a few minutes, star witness and Peter Bacanovic's former assistant, Douglas Faneuil, whose nickname was Baby, took the stand, picking up where testimony left off the day before:

Robert Morvillo: Can you recall how many customers you talked to on that day [December 27, 2001]?

Faneuil: No.

Morvillo: And you can't recall the conversations of any customers that day, is that correct?

Faneuil: Yes.

Morvillo: And you can't recall even the words of one customer, right?

Faneuil: Yes.

Morvillo: But you did talk to Martha Stewart—that you recall, right?

Faneuil: Yes.

And that was how it proceeded: question and answer, question and answer, with the occasional objection until we broke for lunch two hours later. After saying good-bye to Martha out in the hall, Laura and I found Sophie and we walked to Chinatown for dim sum at a restaurant called the Big Wong. We were relieved to be in a room where no one seemed to know English or to be talking about Martha.

Then it was back to the courthouse, where Annie Armstrong, Martha's secretary in her New York office, was to take the stand. Martha was standing up talking to some friends when we reached our seats.

"Lloyd, how long have we known each other?" she asked.

"Oh, about twenty-five years?"

She shook her head. A whiz with dates and numbers, Martha corrected me. "You're wrong. It's twenty-seven years. How are the kids and Leslie? And what are you up to?"

It was funny and kind of surreal talking to her like this standing in the courtroom. Her words and our surroundings made me feel as if it were twenty years earlier, when both of us would have our little chats on those wooden benches at Westport City Hall when we were both in hot water for breaking the local bylaws.

The proceedings began again. Annie, who had been Martha's personal assistant since 1998, seemed visibly shaken as she took the oath. I felt sorry for her up there in the hot seat. She had dark circles under her eyes and looked pale and nervous.

As the prosecution began to take her through the events of one specific day, a day on which Martha had telephoned from Texas, Annie got more and more distressed as she tried to describe the small talk she and Martha exchanged. She told the court that Martha had telephoned her from an airport tarmac on her way to spend a holiday in Mexico. The two had chatted about each other's Christmas holidays.

"I thanked her for the homemade plum pudding she had sent me—" Annie paused on the witness stand, almost wincing, covered her eyes, and began sobbing. As we waited for her to regain composure, someone handed her a tissue. Then she tried again to answer the question, but she burst into tears again, this time louder. Finally, after repeated attempts to continue, the judge dismissed the jury and called it a day, at least two hours earlier than usual. The scene had been dramatic and exhausting.

Laura and I went out to the hallway to hang out with Martha a bit before leaving. Sophie came running up to show her aunt some of the stark black-and-white 11-by-14-inch photos she had taken of her entering the courthouse. Martha studied each one carefully and commended Sophie on her fine technique. She said, "Keep up the good work!"

It was a strange moment. I asked Martha what she thought of Annie's emotional outburst on the stand. "Well," Martha said, deadpan, "I sure am glad I made plum pudding that year for Christmas gifts!"

Martha's close friends were less humorous about what was going on. "It's a tragedy," says Eva. "For anyone to be a victim of this is definitely tragic, but of all the people in the world. . . . It kills me that the world has let her down like this. She has been betrayed by different people because of so much jealousy. And the fact that someone could betray her now—it breaks my heart."

Eva confides that despite Martha's air of confidence, she has moments at home when she lets down the armor. "She gets very teary-eyed," says Eva, well aware that Martha was devastated that her friend Carolyn was near death.

"There was sadness at the company," says Judy Morris. "Carolyn was getting sicker and Martha might be going to jail and the television show would be no more. All of these amazing memories after the past ten years were just finished. It was a lot to digest and to handle. I don't think people fully understand how the company is like a family. Everyone at the company was being affected by all this."

Making a reference to the juror who had lied in his background check and said publicly that he believed Martha's guilty verdict was a "victory for the little guy," Eva says, "It was disgusting to me because all she does is help the little guy. She has created things so that the little guy can have beauty."

Lisa adds, "During the last several months of shooting the television show, we wanted to try to make the show stronger for the stations that still had us on. We had to call people to come on the show. We ended up calling the true friends of the show who were big Martha supporters, and they came just to support her. It was an awkward time to be there—you weren't sure if something might happen and the show might get canceled. But there were a lot of people out there who would do anything for Martha. These were people whose businesses changed because of the exposure they got."

During the trial, Martha endured scrutiny from the media on everything from her clothes to her handbags. Eva tells a story:

Martha is very particular about never having her clothes drag on the floor or hang too long outside of a dry cleaning bag, for example. She's very particular about not putting her purse on the floor of the salon, because who knows what's on the floor. We have an alley cat, Ricky, that lives next door at the deli, and he roams in and out of the neighborhood. Ricky has no tail, he's dirty, and he acts like a dog. He's smart and hilarious.

One morning during the trial Martha was in the salon wearing a three-thousand-dollar Jil Sander suit. She was sitting on one of the chairs in the back. Ricky came in and jumped on top of her and was all over her, licking her neck and putting paw marks all over her. Martha said, "Oh my God, this cat is so *dirty*, this is such a *dirty* little cat!" But she let him crawl all over her. She just dusted the hair and dirt off. She really has a lot of kindness in her.

In March 2004, Martha was found guilty on four counts of obstructing justice and lying to investigators about her stock sale.

Laura called me the next day. She had been chatting with Martha, who had asked her to call me to invite me to come visit her at her TV studio the next day in Norwalk, Connecticut.

They had been in meetings all month about what to do with the show. Indeed, two days after the verdict, Viacom pulled *Martha Stewart Living* completely from its CBS and UPN affiliates. During Martha's trial they had moved the show from its prime daily slot to a less desirable time slot on less desirable stations.

I went to the studios and waited for Martha in one of the offices, a stark white room. She walked in wearing a velour leisure suit and no makeup. She still looked beautiful. We sat down at a table and she gave me an update on the magazine.

"Lloyd, they want to take my name off everything," she said.

"*What*? Martha, you can't do that. That would be the worst thing! You cannot let anyone take your name off anything!"

"There are people here who think I should do just that."

"Stew Leonard stole millions from the government, went to jail, and never once did anyone think to take his name off his stores—and now he's got five more of them." Leonard is a local food retail giant who pled guilty to $17 million in tax fraud in 1993; he repaid the fine while serving a fifty-two-month jail term.

Martha nodded and sat quietly, thinking. She looked down at the table and noticed a spot on the surface, which she rubbed with her finger. "Look how dirty this table is."

"Martha! If they take your name off the magazine, they just don't get it. They don't understand what it's all about."

She nodded, then got up. "Come on. I'll show you around the studio."

As we walked the halls, she was still strong and charismatic, bigger than life and determined to be in control.

Lexi voiced similar thoughts at a board meeting days later. "You should be supporting my mother at this time, not getting scared." But the board was scared and had little faith. They didn't see that all this was just a pause in Martha's career—not the end. Not long after, the board issued a statement that the show was on official hiatus.

"Basically, she was voted off the island," says Lisa. "They were trying to push ahead. The writing was on the wall and it said, it's not about her anymore, we need to keep the company going. People would come up to me and say, 'Ultimately, this is in Martha's best interest. Don't you see? We are trying to save the company!'"

Three weeks later I saw Martha again, but this time, there was no talk of business or sad things. She had invited me over for coffee and dessert after Easter dinner. She greeted me at the door wearing the usual at-home Martha garb—a blue work shirt and white jeans. I gave her a big hug and an extra-tight squeeze of encouragement, then she led me down the diamond-stenciled hallway into the kitchen.

She had laid out a table full of desserts—three different kinds of pie, fruit salad, cookies, and a lemon bundt cake. Everyone was helping himself or herself: her sister Laura and her son Charlie; Martha's niece Sophie and her boyfriend; Sharon Patrick, the president of Martha's company, who would soon become CEO; Suzanne Soble, Martha's marketing director; and, of course, there was Lexi, helping her mother with the plates and coffee cups. Lily, Martha's longtime housekeeper, helped with cleanup.

Notably missing was Martha Senior. There had been a bit of a family tiff that month after Martha's brother Frank announced he was going to auction off sixty of his sister's personal items on eBay, including her first catering car, the black Singer sewing machine she used to make her wedding dress, and the family's double boiler that Martha wrote about in her magazine, describing how the family used to melt chocolate in that pot. Frank was calling the items, which had been in storage since the late eighties, the "Martha Stewart Heritage Authentic Childhood Collection."

It caused a bit of family turmoil, says Martha Kostyra, who takes the blame for the misunderstanding. "I made a big mistake, " she says. "I heard that Frank was selling things that were in the house. I had let him have that stuff because I didn't need it and I was moving. I didn't need the sewing machine anymore because I had another one."

When a reporter called to ask about the auction, "I thought I was doing Martha a big favor, and I said, 'You know, this has nothing to do with Martha. This was just stuff that was mine and I didn't have any use for it. I was moving and I let my son have it because he was finishing his own home in Alabama.' Boy, I never heard the end of it. We call Frank the loose cannon because he did a little too much talking and Martha got mad at him. Family tensions."

The kitchen was different from what I remembered—Martha had enclosed the porch in glass walls—but you could still see a view of the black swimming pool and hear her aviary of songbirds, perched on miniature branches, singing loudly in their cages. Her Himalayan cats were roaming about, and her two chows, as usual, lay on the floor by the back door.

Everyone was avoiding the heavy, somber question on their minds: what was going to happen to Martha? Sentencing was not for another two months and she could face up to five years in jail. Nobody talked about this. We sat and ate forkfuls of delicious dessert, smiling and keeping the conversation light.

After eating, I went along with Martha and some others to take the dogs out for a long walk. As we strolled through her gardens to get to the road, Martha stopped to point out one of her favorite trees. She patted the tree's solid bark. "This tree grows so fast," she said, "no matter what you do to it. It thrives. It's a survivor."

Martha unlocked the iron gate and we all walked out along the deserted street, roaming the neighborhood silently.

9

Another Place to Be Martha

Didn't Julia tell you to bring a *lot* of quarters?

—MARTHA STEWART

If Martha was going to go, she was going to go with a bang, not a whimper.

At the Emmy Awards in May 2004, *Martha Stewart Living* received numerous nominations. The Martha Stewart team had a table reserved at the gala affair. No one was sure if Martha was going to attend or not, so when she did show up, it was pandemonium.

"Martha walked into the huge crowd at the dinner," Lisa Wagner recalls. "The crowd stood up and gave her a standing ovation. It was unbelievable." After the awards, hundreds of fans who had gathered to catch a glimpse of celebrity went wild when they saw Martha. Lisa says, "They were crowding the sidewalks—women of every kind, cheering for Martha, yelling, 'We love you! We're behind you!' It was so great because even though she didn't win the award that night, she saw the people. And they loved her."

Five months later, in October, Martha was preparing to leave for Alderson Federal Prison for Women. She had chosen to get her prison sentence over with sooner rather than later. The day before Martha left, Laura says, "There was no fear or trepidation in her voice. I got the distinct impression that she was just really annoyed that she had to report and waste so many months of her life."

The location of the prison—Alderson, West Virginia—was not what she had asked for. Martha had put in a request for Danbury, Connecticut, since it was much closer to her ninety-three-year-old mother and thirty-eight-year-old daughter.

Meanwhile, the town of Alderson was abuzz with excitement over Martha's impending arrival. As soon as word got out that Martha was on her way, business boomed. The media had arrived nearly two weeks earlier to set up cameras and camp out, taking over the tiny town's one motel.

"You could *feel* that Martha was near," says Betty Alderson, whose family is the namesake of the town and who owns the Alderson Store, a women's clothing store. "Whatever it is about Martha and the aura she projected, her energy and her popularity came ahead of her."

It's not as though Alderson, which holds the distinction of being the first women's prison in the United States and whose nickname is Camp Cupcake, hadn't already seen its share of famous inmates. Billie Holiday spent one year at Alderson for a narcotics violation in 1947, and Manson clan member Lynette "Squeaky" Fromme did time there for pointing a loaded pistol at President Gerald Ford. The cottages at Alderson were meant to re-create the feeling of home life; Alderson had been envisioned as a prison that would retrain its inmates rather than punish them.

Betty says, "My daughter called me when she heard Martha was coming to Alderson and said, 'You've got to do T-shirts and sweatshirts, Mom!'" Betty's daughter knew just what they should say. On the front of the shirt was printed WEST VIRGINIA LIVING, IT'S A GOOD THING. The sweatshirts said LONDON, PARIS, NEW YORK, ALDERSON. Betty made an order for four dozen shirts, and within two days of their and Martha's arrival, they sold out.

Martha arrived at Alderson on October 8, 2004. She was finger-printed and endured a thorough strip search. The guards, wearing latex gloves, checked Martha for lice and ordered her to squat and cough hard so they could check for hidden contraband and drugs.

Martha's clothes and valuables were removed and sent back to Turkey Hill. She was handed her new prison garb: a man's military khaki shirt, a jacket, pants, a plain white T-shirt, and an oversized white cotton T-shirt and men's thermal underwear to sleep in. She was now prisoner number 55170-054.

"They all have to buy the clothes they are going to wear," says Mrs. Kostyra. "Can you imagine? If you want extra food you pay for that, too. Most of the food is government surplus; that's why it's so bad."

Other than being assigned a job in the prison kitchen or becoming an orderly, what was this obsessively overachieving fashion model-turned-stockbroker-turned-homemaker-turned-chief-executive-turned-convict supposed to do for the next five months? It was as if she'd hit a brick wall.

"My mother told me she felt like her life was over," Alexis Stewart told me one day after returning from a prison visit. "She feels the world has let her down."

.   .   .

Soon after her first day there, Martha was already one of the popular inmates, and she began to form her own clique. Her first friend was a Catholic nun who was serving almost three years for involvement in a protest at a missile silo. Then she befriended the woman who ran the dining hall, "Mother Queenpin," who had served twenty-two years of a thirty-year sentence. Then there was her favorite, Susan, who had been at Alderson for twelve years and who became a sort of pet project for Martha.

"She's very attractive and smart, but completely terrified of human attachments," Martha wrote in a letter. "She eats alone and gardens alone." Martha gave Susan one of her own gardening books and Susan began to open up to her. "She read it front to back before talking to me. I also gave her Elliott Coleman's book on organic gardening."

Soon the two were sharing meals together. Martha said of Susan, "She'd pick wild greens from around the prison grounds—dandelions, sorrel, wild onions, and garlic—and share her harvest with me, once picking some strange round leaf that I found delightful." These mixed greens helped supplement the inmates' nothing-to-write-home-about prison food.

Alexis told me of another prisoner who became a friend of Martha's, a young woman who was sentenced to years in prison simply for saying, "I don't know, ask that guy over there" to an undercover agent asking her where he could buy drugs.

.   .   .

Inquisitive, observant, and calculating, Martha took everything in, asked questions, and listened carefully to her fellow inmates. This might have been the first time she ever had both the time and the desire to listen to girlfriends talking about their problems.

Most of the women were in prison because a friend or relative facing a harsh sentence had snitched on them. This did not sit well with Martha. She began firing off letters to a friend at the *Wall Street Journal*. She wrote the letters on the prison typewriter and sent them to her assistant, Julia Eisemann, who then transcribed them verbatim to e-mails and sent them to the *Journal*.

Martha said, "The only problem is that one of the reporters mentioned in their article that I had e-mailed from inside the prison. I've got to tell Julia to tell them they can't say that sort of thing or I'll be in *big* trouble."

Other inmates were prostitutes, drug addicts, petty criminals, and unfit mothers. Now they had a major celebrity in their midst who was ready to dispense advice, and Martha couldn't stop herself from giving it.

"These women have so much less than us," Martha said. "They need my help. They're people—not any different from us. The system is failing them. They want to be productive but don't know how."

As the holidays approached, Martha and the other inmates decorated the administration building using anything and everything they could find around the 75-acre camp. She and the others fashioned a wreath of spruce measuring almost 40 inches in diameter. They decorated it with freshly fallen pinecones and some red balls that were left over from other decorations—wreaths, swags, and Christmas trees.

Martha gathered the troops together to make a holly wreath for the officer who ran the fix-it shop as well. When the prisoners hung it up in his window, it sagged. Distressed by this malfunction, Martha pointed it out to the officer, who made her a large metal ring to keep the wreath upright. Martha would have made it herself, of course, but the inmates were not permitted near tools, much less allowed to use them.

The wreath garnered admiration among the prison staff, and Martha hoped the crew would get a bonus for their work. The average pay for most was $15 a month for the chores they performed in the prison, including raking leaves, bathroom duty, and laundry detail. Martha was a hit on bathroom duty, and at one point she instructed all the women how to properly clean the floor waxer so the floors would shine better.

To make extra money, some inmates worked as manicurists or hairstylists at the prison. Others had relatives on the outside who would send the $290 monthly allotment allowed each prisoner for use in the commissary to buy sundries such as toothpaste, soap, yarn, shoes, a deck of cards, or cigarettes.

Most did not have those people on the outside, and Martha felt sorry for them. During one phone call with her executive assistant, Julia, she tried to remedy the situation. "Julia, do you think we can arrange for deposits of $290 to go into some inmates' bank accounts?"

"Ms. Stewart, hang up this phone this instant!" said a stern voice listening in on the call. The prison phone cop had been monitoring her conversation.

.   .   .

Martha was allowed visitors four out of seven days, and except for the immediate family, the visits were divided into morning or afternoon sessions, four hours from eight to twelve or from twelve to four. In the beginning, her visitors were an inconsistent trickle and she complained about that.

"She's driving me nuts," Alexis told me one day after one of her weekend visits to her mother. Alexis made the ten-hour drive from Connecticut each weekend, listening to audiobooks on the way. "She wants to see more people. She's lonely and bored. I go down and visit her for days at a time and sit and listen to her and eat that crappy food. There is positively nothing to eat in that town. *Nothing!*"

You'd have to understand Lexi's wicked sense of humor to know how devoted she was and how she was only joking around when she'd say things like "I refuse to go down next weekend; I need a break," or "I told my mother I wasn't coming back down for Thanksgiving."

It wasn't long before Martha was fielding visits like any other set of appointments. Eventually, Julia, with her wonderfully precise English accent, instructed each and every person planning to make the trek: "Once you've made a date to visit Martha, please try to honor that date so the day will not be vacant and others scrambling to fill it. And it's best to eat before you visit. There is no real food, no real coffee or tea. Unless you want an excuse to gorge on candy bars—in that case, you're all set. Take a lot of quarters for the vending machines. Leave anything you can't take in in the car; there are no lockers. And don't forget to wear warm clothes. It's cold in that prison."

I visited Alderson with Laura at Martha's behest. "I would love to see you," Martha said in an e-mail message sent by Julia. "We have lots to talk about. It will be a fun day!"

It was a quiet wintry evening when we arrived in that remote Appalachian valley. It snowed lightly as we drove down the mountains. We made our way to the Hospitality House for Alderson, a rustic old home that accommodated visitors with limited means of support—shelter and food were provided at no charge. Nondenominational religious services were available, too. We weren't spending the night there; we went to pick up a key to the house where we would stay that Betty Alderson lent us.

Sophie Herbert had recently stayed at the Hospitality House during a visit to Martha and she reported to her that it was lacking in Martha-like necessities: quality sheets, blankets, towels, and other comforts. Martha immediately directed Julia to send what was needed to the House. Although the House is still not exactly the Ritz, it is now fully decked out in Martha Everyday from Kmart.

Early the next morning, we passed through various checkpoints and arrived at a 12-by-12-foot freestanding small brick building where we had to line up with other visitors. Once inside the cramped quarters, we each filled out a form and had to list whom we were visiting, that person's prison number, and the license plate number, make, and model of the car we were driving. The next step was to go to the visitors' hall and wait until the guard at the desk checked us in.

"Are you staying for count?" the guard asked, referring to four P.M., the time the prisoners were counted. This old tradition dates back to the earliest days at Alderson. Up until very recently, they rang bells to signal the beginning and end of count. There were five counts per day. "If your arrival is too close to one of the counts, you won't be allowed in until after all inmates are accounted for," the clerk told us in a tone that let you know he'd given this speech a thousand times. "Once you get inside the prison, you can't leave," he warned us. "No going out to your car. If you do, your visit is over."

"I don't think we'll be down for the count," I said, trying for a little humor.

The guard was not amused. He took our forms and the clear plastic bags we were given to keep our ID and any other items that were allowed into the prison—prescriptions, cigarettes (new, unopened packs only), lighters, quarters for the vending machines, eyeglasses or sunglasses, and makeup.

On the morning of our visit, one of the guards told us that Martha had awakened early and had volunteered to shovel the snow from the prison sidewalks. "I'd be doing just the same if I were back in Westport!" she told them cheerily and got to work. "It's good exercise."

Martha entering the visitors' room was a sight to behold. In she purposefully strode, with her khaki pants and shirt perfectly pressed. Her khaki overshirt was unbuttoned and worn like a jacket, revealing a white cotton T-shirt underneath. Her hair was impeccably groomed, and she was wearing sunglasses that looked decidedly European.

As she walked in, she motioned to Laura and me to move over to a particular set of chairs. "Grab those. They're the best seats in the house," she said. After hugs and kisses, she explained why. First, from the vantage point of that particular table, she had a clear view of the whole room. This was important lest someone sneak a photo of her—the press had been relentless, and the tabloids were offering people in the town $1,000 a pop for any information or photos of Martha. Second, the seat gave her access to the light switches for the room as well as control of the ceiling fan and heating thermostat, to which she made adjustments occasionally as we spoke, scouting the room first to make sure no guard was watching. Then we moved right to the important topic—the drama of prison life.

Martha told us a story about how she'd almost been in a scuffle a few nights before. She had been swept up in an intense Scrabble game with a few others in the recreation hall when she was pelted from behind with a cascade of dominoes. Annoyed, the players turned to see who had interfered with their game. It was a woman sitting in the corner who looked as if she either had taken a shine to Martha or wanted to start a fight with her. Either way, she looked menacing.

"Lay off her!" one inmate in the Scrabble game yelled at the domino thrower.

"I was just blowing off steam," said the woman. "I didn't mean to hit you *personally*," she said to Martha.

The women huddled back around their game in a circle around Martha and the playing resumed, the potential fight averted.

"The women looked out for her," says Eva Scrivo, who also visited Martha in prison. "All the things that make people different—age, social status, wealth, poverty—none of that matters to Martha. Being thrown into this prison environment, she discovered that there were educated women, uneducated women, women who couldn't raise their children—all kinds."

As Martha's colorist for several years, Eva says, "The first thing I did when I got there was look at her hair color. Martha had been doing her own highlights in prison. It wasn't bad. She looked well rested and vibrant and she was making the best of it. She wanted to know what was up with me. She did not feel sorry for herself at all."

Martha told us she bonded with many of the inmates by teaching them her own personal Martha Stewart Living health and beauty tips, free of charge. "Your hair will fall out if you keep braiding it," she had warned one African American friend. "You've got to stop."

Martha and her new friends also discussed nutrition—she tried to get everybody on a health kick with her, eschewing the high-fat foods served in the cafeteria and foraging with other inmates for as many greens as they could find on the grounds.

Martha skipped lunch while in prison and began teaching evening yoga classes to a dozen regular students. "I think many of the women have been rejuvenated," Martha said, " simply having me around." (When I later told Martha's mother this, she was amazed. "I had no idea my daughter could teach yoga," she said.)

And even though the food wasn't much to write home about, Martha did. In a typewritten note that Julia e-mailed to friends and family, Martha wrote:

For breakfast this weekend there was a rather simple but good meal. Two hard-boiled eggs—they must have read *MSL* because they were delicious—just a tad soft in the middle and tender whites—whole wheat toast—although I had to look for the very scant amount of wheat in the bread, real butter doled out with a minuscule ice cream scoop, watery coffee, with 2% milk, that actually tasted like coffee and a bright orange clementine. I felt as if I were at Turkey Hill eating one of my own hard-boiled eggs, sliced and laid on buttered toast.

Martha learned a few beauty tips herself while in jail. "Laura, you have to go home and try every product you can find," Martha said to her sister excitedly about one newly discovered brand she had found in the prison commissary.

Martha pointed to a new pair of boots on her feet and complained, "These cost me six hundred hours of labor! Sixty-five dollars! I found the Wal-Mart price tag inside one of the shoes. Guess what the price was? *Thirty-five dollars*! I took the tag back to them and let them know what a rip-off it was." Even Martha's bark couldn't get the prison people to back down on the price. They were, however, rather stylish ankle-high boots, and she wore them untied in a casual manner, with the tongues pulled out and away—the way kids sometimes wear sneakers.

At a certain point during our visit, Martha leaned back in her chair, stretched out her legs, raised them, then let her heels hit the ground, proclaiming, "I think I'll have an orange juice." This was our cue to get out our quarters and fetch a refreshment for her from the vending machine. Unfortunately, this was one rule of Julia's we had not heeded closely enough.

When Martha discovered we had only three quarters between us, she gave us a mild scolding. "Didn't Julia tell you to bring a *lot* of quarters?"

I went to the machines and inserted a dollar in the change machine only to find it was out of change. I then put my dollar into another vending machine and found the orange juice was out of stock, but I managed to get my money returned in quarters, thank God. I was able to get Martha her orange juice from yet another machine in the long row of machines.

I went back and handed her the coveted juice. She leaned over, adjusted the speed of the overhead fan, sat back in her chair, then took a long, cool gulp.

"Lloyd, I think I'm going to get the chef over at Le Cirque to come stay at the house and cook my meals for me when I get out of here," she said, then sipped more restorative juice.

Martha and her fellow inmates were allotted 300 minutes of phone time per month, and besides calls with her mother and Lexi, Martha used up her minutes with Julia, her lifeline to the rest of the world. They spoke almost every day so Martha could get constant updates on what was going on at the office.

Every day Julia prepared an express package for overnight delivery to Alderson, which took two days to get there—the town was so remote it required an extra day in transit. Federal Express packages were forbidden; the prison only accepted mail from the United States Postal Service.

Besides money, books of stamps are common currency in jail. It didn't take long for Martha to learn to use the bartering system to get what she wanted. In exchange for a book of stamps, $2 in yarn, and a bag of fiberfill, Martha commissioned a fellow inmate to crochet Christmas presents for the seven cats waiting for her back home. A few weeks later, the job was done and Martha was presented with seven woolly rats.

"They are so adorable! And my, they each have a different expression!"

Next she worried about what she was going to do for presents for her dogs. Everyone at Alderson was all booked up with holiday needlework, so Martha decided she would make them herself. She had mastered the single and double stitch from her mother, but Martha has always preferred knitting. Nevertheless, she decided to crochet a large gray and pink possum for each dog.

First she checked the encyclopedia in the prison library to find the correct shape and color of the nocturnal creature. Trying to find the exact shade of yarn proved more difficult. Martha told us, "The assortment of yarn at Alderson is really quite sad."

It was while looking for the gray shade that she came across a type of yarn that was new to her. "It was actually more of a cotton string, and when doubled it creates a wonderful texture," she described. "You wouldn't believe the color—it was exact Hermès orange, just like the Hermès boxes, and spectacular. I am going to crochet the scarf of all scarves for Kevin, Mr. Hermès himself."

She was referring to Kevin Sharkey, the editorial director of decorating at *Martha Stewart Living*. Martha qualified this by saying that due to the rate at which she was crocheting, she might have to make the scarf an Easter gift instead of a Christmas one.

"But I know if I put my mind to it, I could progress, I could improve."

If only Mr. Hermès could have seen Martha do her stuff in prison, I thought. As the holidays approached, the inmates held a decorating contest with a cash prize of $100 to go to the cottage judged best decorated. The theme was Peace on Earth. Everyone in Martha's cottage, J11, looked to her for guidance.

"They're all relying on me, so I have to give it a try," she confided. "And there's not much to work with around here."

There was nothing like a little competition to make Martha feel like Martha. She knew how to write the word *peace* in about a hundred languages. So with approximately $25 worth of glue and glitter, ribbons and construction paper, she decided they'd make white banners, furled at the ends, and would hang them from the ceiling, each one inscribed with *peace* in a different language.

Martha had even more up her sleeve. Using some of her valuable phone minutes, she rang up Julia and asked her if she'd seen any inspiring holiday decorations about town. Julia told her about the ad for Tiffany she'd seen in the *Wall Street Journal* with stars made from wreaths of flying birds. That was it, Martha decided; she was going to bring a little Tiffany to Alderson. She asked Julia to send her the advertisement along with instructions on how to fold doves and cranes origami-style.

"We have to be so careful," Martha told her comrades when the goods arrived in the mail. "Somebody asked me the other day how to fold an origami crane. Her girlfriend lives across the hall, so she obviously leaked our theme to the other group!"

Not only had the theme been leaked, but the eventual outcome of the contest would later be leaked as well. Newspaper headlines read along the lines of STEWART UNABLE TO LEAD TEAM TO VICTORY. The press found it irresistible to report that a competing cottage won the contest by constructing a nativity scene with snow-covered hills, sleds, and clouds.

·   ·   ·

For the final hour of our four-hour visit with Martha, we played Scrabble. A four-hour jail visit is a long time, and you run out of things to talk about. There was only so much Laura and I could report from the outside world and only so much Martha could tell us about the inside. So out came the Scrabble board from the shelf in the visitors' room.

Martha had come armed with her dog-eared *Official Scrabble Dictionary* so she could challenge us on any words that we put down that looked suspect. Martha has been an avid Scrabble player since childhood. Her father taught her the basics of the game. She told me that she prefers to play with more than one other person because the game is over quicker that way. She kept score with a pencil and notepad. She took the lead from the beginning, getting one bingo (a seven-letter word) and two triple-word scores, and playing a doozy off my dismal *x* word.

"Lloyd, you have *got* to learn all the two-letter words that start with *x*," she scolded. In the end, she beat me by only six points.

"She doesn't like to play with me," Alexis told me, "because she can't bear to lose, which she often does when we play together."

Martha likes to win.

Back in Westport after my prison pilgrimage, I went by the house on Turkey Hill Road to pass along the news of my visit with Martha. Her mother was holding down the fort along with the maid, Lily. They watched over the house, the seven cats, the two dogs, and the innumerable songbirds. Martha had been calling her mother regularly to check in and always asked, "Are you petting the cats and dogs?"

The two chows greeted me as usual in flat-out reclining positions on the floor of the back entryway. The cats were everywhere, many with their crocheted rats that Martha's friend had made; some of the toys were missing ears and their yarn was unraveling. One of the dogs' pink-bellied possums was sprawled on the kitchen table.

Holding up her fist and making a muscle in her arm, Lily asked, "How is Martha? Strong?" Martha's mother laughed.

I responded, "Like a bull!"

Martha's mother had made a visit to her daughter on Thanksgiving Day with Laura; Laura's husband, Randy; their son, Charlie; and their daughter, Sophie. "It was heartbreaking to me that my grandmother of over ninety had to spend Thanksgiving in prison," says Sophie. "That was the hardest thing for me."

Before they even got to see Martha, there had been delays. "I had forgotten my driver's license for ID at the hotel," says Laura. "It was a thirty-five-minute drive away. Stupidly, I had left it in my other jacket and they were giving me a hard time about letting me in. I had to prove somehow that I was Martha's sister. Martha couldn't understand why they were making her wait so long to come in and see us. We had to wait in the long line. Martha's little place was the next building over. She could see us and was waving to us—then all of a sudden she stepped back and there were ten other ladies waving to us!"

Once her family got to her, they were glad to find Martha in good spirits. "She was very happy on Thanksgiving," says Laura.

Though Sophie was at first struck by the reality of being in a prison—"It was a harsh and emotional place," she says—she was also moved by the experience. "It was nice in a way, having everything taken away, not having the distractions of a big family dinner. It was simple and we were thrown in with a bunch of people we didn't know in a big room. But it was a real honest place to be. I thought to myself, no one has died, no one is ill, and everyone is learning from this experience."

As the visit ended, "the hardest part was saying good-bye," says Mrs. Kostyra. "Everyone shed lots and lots of tears. You know — the kids and husbands knowing it would be a long time until another visit."

When Sophie left the prison that day, she and Charlie heard some heartfelt words from Aunt Martha. "There are people who will die in this prison and won't ever get a visit from the outside, and that is so sad," she told her niece and nephew. "I hope you will always have the will to learn, to imagine, and to see."

When the family left the prison, they were starving. The problem with visiting Alderson on a holiday was that all the vending machines that were normally packed with candy, popcorn, pizza, and other nonholiday fare were empty before noon with all the family visiting going on. Sophie went back to Hospitality House, where she had stayed the night before. "I ended up cooking Thanksgiving dinner with everyone at the house," she says. "I loved that place. I didn't tell them who I was, but they figured it out."

Laura, Randy, and Charlie went looking for a restaurant, but the only place open was the local Wal-Mart. Laura says, "We went to Wal-Mart hoping to find something to eat there. I stood there thinking what a bizarre Thanksgiving this was. Prison in the morning, Wal-Mart in the afternoon — and then somebody tapped my shoulder." It was Laura's nephew, Kirk, George's son, who had also come down to visit Martha with George and the rest of the family. They, too, had come to Wal-Mart looking for something to eat. "It seems that next to the prison, Wal-Mart was the most happening place in Alderson," Laura says.

Alderson might have said a silent prayer of thanks to Martha for Wal-Mart's being open that day. Before Martha got there, "the town was a quiet, subdued little town, not a whole lot going on," says Betty Alderson. She continues:

It's hard to keep a business going because we don't have enough traffic. But even before Martha got here, we almost became a bustling little town. So many people came from all over. Many of them thought they could just pop into town and go over and visit her. And if they couldn't do that, at least they wanted to get as close to her as possible, so they would drive down to the prison gate or cross the river and look across where they could see into the prison. Of course, when all these people were in town they would come and shop at all the stores in Alderson, stay at the motel, and eat in the restaurants, so it was a great boon to Alderson. It put us on the map, and the media was so kind. They portrayed us in a very positive way. We have nice people, and it's a pretty little town.

Martha's friends came to town, some of them in a limousine, and that was a big thing for Alderson. We watched for that limo to come into town every day, and then Martha's friends would come into the store once in a while and they would say, "Martha sent us."

In honor of Martha, Betty set up a shrine of sorts in her store: a display of Martha's books stacked on a pretty lace tablecloth surrounded by a tea set of china cups and saucers. "I was overwhelmed with Martha's generosity and her doing what she did for us," Betty says. "I became a big Martha fan. We saw a softer side to Martha. We saw why she became the person that she is because she not only worked very hard but she projected a lot of good things."

After Martha left, the town just wasn't the same, says Betty. "I felt a big void," she told me. "I thought, how can we go back to being that slow little town again? But the media still comes in every now and then to ask us how Alderson is after Martha. It is much slower, but we are still feeling the effects of her being here."

Whether Martha knows it nor not, she left something behind, something that will live on in the tiny town that grew to love the big CEO from New York. "A lady came in and gave me some of Martha's crocuses," says Betty with a smile, "so I planted some over at my house and I gave some out to other people to plant at theirs. So now we'll all have a constant beautiful reminder that Martha was once here."

10

Back Home

It just seemed like the natural thing to do.

—ALEXIS STEWART

etty Alderson was among the small crowd of town residents who gathered on the tarmac shortly after two A.M. on March 4, 2005, at Greenbrier Valley Airport, seventeen miles from the prison, to say good-bye to Martha. As Martha and Lexi boarded the private company jet together, one resident waved a sign that said, WE'LL MISS YOU MARTHA! GOOD LUCK! COME BACK AND VISIT US! Betty and others waved. Martha, decked out in a poncho a fellow inmate had crocheted for her out of the gray yarn from the prison commissary, waved back.

A few hours later she was back at her new home in Bedford, New York, frustrating the paparazzi camped out at her front gate as she drove in behind tinted car windows. The cameras could not get a clear shot of her, which was just as well, because she was not picture-ready just yet. Martha already had a Friday night date planned that would prepare her for the cameras — Eva Scrivo was coming over to do her highlights.

As Eva mixed the highlighting solutions and got her scissors ready to give Martha the full beauty treatment in the kitchen, Lexi made her famous risotto for Martha's first home-cooked meal after months of prison food. Eva says:

> We had dinner with close friends while she had her high-lighting liquid on and it was funny because we were working with hardly any light. The house was behind in renovation and construction. So we had actually taken a lamp and removed the shade—anything for light. It's so funny that people get nervous around Martha like she's this perfectionist and expects the best, because we've been in the funniest of circumstances.
>
> One time we filmed a commercial in a cotton field in Texas. It was when cotton sheets were first introduced to Kmart. It was something like a hundred degrees. They had taken a bed and put it in the middle of a cotton field. I was dreading the job because of the heat—that is not an environment for great hair and makeup. We shot for about sixteen hours, and Martha remained flawless out there. She's that resilient.

In the months while Martha was in prison, Alexis and Laura's husband, Randy, were in charge of preparing Martha's Bedford home for her arrival. Martha wasn't there while the work went on, of course, so that was frustrating for her. But she had seen pictures of the floor in the main building. Alexis and Randy were furious when they found out that she was using a friend to go to the house and photograph the work in progress for her. But

Martha is Martha and details are her obsession. In one of Martha's many letters to her mother, she wrote, "Mother—are all the doorknobs polished and nice and shiny?"

During my visit to the prison, Martha had been unable to contain her excitement when she talked about her new home in Bedford. She urged me to take my family for a visit. She spoke of the concrete slabs in the horse stable that had been textured to look like wood. "It took me three years to find the woman who could do the process," Martha told me. "She uses large hand-held metal forms and presses the design into the wet cement."

Now that she was home, she saw there was much more work to be done before it met with her approval. Her first morning home, in the clear light of day, Martha strolled through the house and inspected it, making a list of work that still needed to be completed—a scratch was on this wall, this paint finish wasn't quite right, this molding needed to be replaced, and on and on. Now that she was under house arrest, she was going to be spending far more time than usual at home and would be even keener on the details.

Some family came over the next night for dinner. Martha cooked. On Sunday, Martha threw her first official postprison party.

"It was a very small gathering of close friends and family," says Lisa Wagner, who took her three sons. "It was quite a day, just to see her in the new house." Martha had laid out a buffet and rustic baskets full of thick bread on the two-inch-thick white marble countertop in her kitchen. Next to the white flat soup bowls and plates, she adorned the table with glass vases filled with white calla lilies, tight-budded irises, and white tulips. On the windowsills she had placed white pots of fragrant pink and lavender hyacinths.

"The kids thought it was great that Martha offered Coke in those small old-fashioned glass bottles," says Lisa. Coca-Cola was a drink Martha had learned to appreciate at Alderson. "It was just like old times. Martha showed everyone around the property. She was so overjoyed to see everyone."

After a good night's sleep, Martha was gracious to the press gang outside and mixed them up batches of lemonade and hot cocoa.

"I think that going through the experience that she had gone through allowed her to get in touch with herself and how she really feels inside." says Eva. "Martha is very outgoing, and when she came home I think she just acted true to herself. She was engaging with the press. She realized that the best thing to do is just be who you are, so she was generous and friendly with all the newsmen and women. She had a very healthy attitude about everything."

Martha accepted the fact that the press—and the world— were going to be curious about how and what she was doing, how she looked, and what her next big step was going to be.

Martha was back and soon everything was like before—a frenzy. For those who thought she'd sit back and take a rest and be a different kind of Martha—a quieter, meeker, softer kind of Martha—forget it. "When she comes back, *watch out*," Laura had told me just before her release. "Martha has two years of her life to make up for."

She wanted that house finished, and fast. So she pushed the construction workers, who were behind schedule, to complet the job in the same way she always pushed her workers. After months working with the big boss out of town, this was their first time getting the full Martha treatment. Long hours and hard work were the order of the day both inside and outside the house.

Martha managed to create an oasis. As soon as the greenhouse out back was finished, Martha filled it with exotic fruit trees and plants.

Besides housework, there was other business to tend to. Martha held a press conference at her Omnimedia headquarters, praising her more than six hundred employees. She got to work on her two new television shows, various book deals, and wrapping up her new baking cookbook that Lisa and others had worked on in her absence. Martha busied herself with business meetings at home, dinner parties, and other gatherings.

One day she had her mother over to lunch when she was entertaining ninety-year-old David Rockefeller as one of her guests. "He was such a nice man," said Mrs. Kostyra afterward. "It's so good to have her back. Martha was saying that the ankle bracelet was cutting into her ankle and hurting her. Of course, she doesn't like any restrictions. Down in Virginia, she had to stay put but she was able to move around. Here, even though she was in her own element, she couldn't move around. She didn't have the freedom. That was part of the punishment, you know. What could you do? You had to accept it."

Martha had some mishaps with the ankle bracelet from the beginning. Her parole officer had forgotten to tell her that they needed a separate telephone line for transmitting signals from the ankle bracelet, so Randy had to do some fast maneuvering to prepare for the day they hooked it on her leg.

Knowing Martha, I knew the ankle bracelet would prove to be almost more of a prison to her than the previous five months. She simply couldn't stand the bracelet.

Alexis told me that the bracelet was all about power, the trial was about power, putting her away was about power—and most of all, not letting her work was all about power. "She couldn't work as much as she wanted," said Alexis. "They could come and bust her and she would be in violation of her probation."

Martha could leave the house for only forty-eight hours a week to go to work and also to work in her garden. She put the hours to the best use she could.

I had known of Martha's meeting with the reality TV producer Mark Burnett long before the announcement of the big new TV shows. He had been up at Martha's home in Maine for a weekend visit before she even left for prison. It was information I had to keep to myself.

I also had heard about the Sirius Satellite deal way in advance. When Howard Stern was signed way back when, I said to myself, satellite radio won't get serious until they sign Martha, and sure enough my premonition came true.

Martha and Lexi ran themselves ragged in the eight-week shoot for *The Apprentice: Martha Stewart*, which debuted on September 21, 2005.

"How did your mother convince you to do it?" I asked Lexi. "You never liked to be in the spotlight."

Lexi shrugged. "It just seemed like the natural thing to do. We had a lot of fun together. We shot one scene where there was an exchange between me and my mother and I made a sort of sarcastic remark to my mom. One of the contestants blurted out, 'I'll bet that wasn't in the script!'"

I made a remark about someone else who had a famous person as a parent and how it was difficult for that person at times. "Tell me about it!" Alexis said, and we both laughed. During our e-mails throughout the shoot, Lexi wrote that one beauty routine that became indispensable after a long day on the set was her at-home massages—or as she put it, "my two-hour *torture* massages."

"Overall, the *Apprentice* experience was all right," Lexi added. "I just hated the waiting-around part."

Though she worked herself to the bone, Martha reveled in being back to work. "The contestants were in awe of Martha," Eva told me. "They wanted to do anything to please her. Everyone was bowled over by her charisma.

"I think by the third day on the set Martha was in the swing of things. She had it down. Everyone was playing off each other and it was magic. Alexis brought in the young point of view and also the dynamic between Martha and herself. It was fun."

When she was not working, Martha was busy making up for lost time with her daughter and enjoying her gardens and her prized horses. Lexi says:

The other day she put me on a horse and wanted me to take a ride. The horse took off in a gallop and it threw me off. I asked her, "What's the name of that horse?" My mother said, "Dirt," and I said, "*Dirt*! You put me on a horse named Dirt?"

During the trial I saw a friend on the street who hadn't seen me in a couple of years. He had seen me on TV and commented on how much closer my mother and I seemed to be. I said, "What are you talking about?"

My mother and I have *always* been close. We are not closer since the trial and prison—we've always been close. I talk to my mother at least once a day, *every* day. I was going to be there for her and I was happy to do it. She would be there for me if the situation were reversed, but it doesn't mean we are any closer than before. When would we have time to sit with each other five days a week and do nothing except be tortured?

Sometimes we fight, sometimes we don't. Sometimes we hang out together and other times we don't. Big deal. It was certainly a time for me to be with my mother. It would have been incomprehensible if I hadn't been there for her.

Martha jumped right into planning and getting ready for her other show, *Martha,* a daily show shot before a live audience. One day I viewed the promos. One clip showed Martha being knocked over by a cow—I remember that incident from an Easter egg hunt shoot she did at Turkey Hill a decade ago—and I knew she was going to have another hit on her hands.

Lisa, who oversees content on the show, says:

Everyone is so excited. We are working to do something very different, and it just feels right. We have our core viewers, but a huge part of what we're doing is to reach out to more new viewers. There are a lot of people who now know about Martha but they don't really know much about her—or they didn't watch the old show.

She's back in a role that feels a lot less perfect and a lot funnier. It's a how-to show, but with more entertainment. People who know Martha well know that she has a good sense of humor—we've all seen it over the years. The new show is relatable to many more people.

Just like old times, Martha Senior made an early appearance on *Martha*. Mrs. Kostyra told me in July 2005 during one of our get-togethers, "I have no idea what I'm going to do. All I know is I'm to have my hair done and my nails done and my clothes done. They're picking me up, so I don't have to worry about driving and parking. I'm willing to do it. Martha is working so hard on it. She said to me, 'Oh mother, it's so much work.' But we haven't had time to talk about it. She's always busy doing something."

The mood on the set is upbeat, says Lisa. Martha has fun as they shoot. "I have to say I'm really glad to be back here working for her. It's in a different office. We're in the city now. We've built a new studio, the largest live TV studio ever built! A new chapter is being written. You can feel that the company is working to regain its strength and momentum. Everything feels like it makes perfect sense. The time that I wasn't there I always knew I'd be back—it was just a hiatus. Martha has a lot of confidence in her key people and having them around her. That is really important to her. It's really important that the show still delivers valuable content and that's never going to change. That is always going to be the most important thing to Martha, and her readers and viewers expect quality."

A few weeks after she got out of prison, Martha gave her former assistant, Judy Morris, a call to check in and rally the troops back together. She didn't sound quite like the boss of old. Judy explains:

> The phone rang, and it was Martha. She said, "How are you doing? I just wanted to check in. We'll stay in touch. Everything is going to be okay. And we're all going to be back together again."
>
> She wanted to see what I was up to, what I wanted to do to be a part of the company, and where I was with the new baby and the family. I told her my concerns about my being in Weston — it's a longer commute. I have these two kids and I was a bit worried. As much as I would love to work for her every single day and be a part of the whole excitement of the new show, I felt like it was way too much for me to do with the family. I told her that I was interested in something part time, though.
>
> Martha was very understanding and very open to it and said, "We'll work something out. Don't worry about it."
>
> She called back and invited us over to her house for Easter Sunday in Bedford — my husband, the two kids, and me. I hadn't seen her in a year and it was like I just saw her yesterday. Immediately she gave me a big hug and a kiss and she grabbed Eddie, my baby, and walked around with

him. She took a bunch of us on a tour through the greenhouse. She was so proud of it and showed us all the different plants and fruit trees.

Our three-year-old son, Jimmy, was skipping along with her in the greenhouse. She picked a kumquat and gave it to him as well as a little Meyer lemon to suck on. He kept sticking all these exotic fruits in his pocket.

As we were driving away, we looked back. Martha and Lexi went off on a walk out into this beautiful field, on a gorgeous afternoon. It was just so amazing to see her and her daughter together. Lexi has stood by her mother with all that she had to go through. Lexi had to be so strong, and she was there for her.

Lexi is amazed at how much her mother is lapping up her postprison attention and doesn't mind one bit that the media and the neighbors are just a few feet away from her living space.

"When I went to Bedford for the first time, I told her to knock it all down and start over, but no, she couldn't do that," Lexi said one day. "And now she lives in a house twenty feet from the road!"

"What's she going to do now, raise the stone wall?" I asked.

"No, it's against town regulations."

"Oh, God—you don't want her to get in trouble with the town like the old days!"

"No, and besides, she enjoys being famous. She likes the attention she's been getting."

.   .   .

I don't believe the women Martha met in prison will ever leave her mind and heart. When she left prison, she wrote this on her Web site:

> Someday, I hope to have the chance to talk more about all that has happened, the extraordinary people I have met here and all that I have learned. I can tell you now that I feel very fortunate to have had a family that nurtured me, the advantage of an excellent education, and the opportunity to pursue the American dream. You can be sure that I will never forget the friends that I met here, all that they have done to help me over these five months, their children, and the stories they have told me.

There is disagreement among family and friends as to whether Martha has "changed" since prison.

In July 2005, Sophie Herbert visited her aunt in Bedford to have some quality time with her for the first time since she had gotten out of prison. Sophie herself had been on a sort of year-long spiritual quest, spending months traveling in India and going on retreat, trying to make sense of the past year and what her aunt went through.

Maybe Martha *had* changed a bit in jail—if so, Sophie would be someone who could really see it—but jail was the furthest thing from both their minds when Sophie arrived for her visit. She had hitched a ride with some friends, and when they dropped her off, Martha invited everyone in for a gourmet dinner cooked by her Le Cirque chef. After dinner, she gave them all a tour of the grounds.

When the guests left, Martha and Sophie settled into the couch and put on a DVD of *The Merchant of Venice*. Next to Martha were her dogs and the crocheted rats and possums made in prison.

"It was so funny," Sophie told me. "Martha fell asleep in her chair with her black French bulldog, Francesca, the one that sleeps in her bed with her. And during the movie, they both fell asleep and the bulldog was snoring away."

Martha was finally home, and it was a Good Thing.

11

Moving Forward

fter the *Apprentice* shoot wrapped, I had afternoon tea with Lexi. We met at her ultramodern penthouse apartment on the fringes of Tribeca, an ultrachic downtown neighborhood in Manhattan. Lexi's apartment is decorated in stark contrast to the rustic style she grew up with at Turkey Hill. The rooms are sleek and gray with brushed aluminum and leather furniture, and there is not a wicker basket in sight. Still, visiting Lexi was reminiscent of my early days visiting Martha.

"I'm baking cakes. Come on into the kitchen," she said. She was wearing striped jogging pants and a tank top and her hair still had the strawberry blond highlights she had added for *The Apprentice*. I could see remnants of makeup on her usually bare face from the day's shoot for the show's finale.

"Makeup! You're more beautiful without it, you know," I said. She laughed as she leaned toward the hot oven and turned her three bundt cakes exactly 180 degrees, just the way her mother taught her.

"I guess it's part of my new corporate image," she said with her trademark irony.

Whatever, Alexis looked great. She poured me a mug of herbal tea and sat down at the kitchen table with a little sigh. She was more than ready for a vacation, she said, and planned a week-long rest in Maine.

"Maybe I can't run away," she said. "There's too much work to be done. But I can have the fantasy. Hey, do you know of any good yoga teachers? I'm looking for a few who we can interview for the satellite radio show."

I gave her the names of a few local yoga studios. She jotted them down before moving to the stove. She took the cakes out of the oven and put them on a rack to cool.

"I wonder how the town of Alderson is doing," I mused.

"I hear they are going to plant a garden there in my mother's honor," she said. We both laughed, thinking it was very fitting.

Thank goodness, Martha returned to society. I plan on being there every step of the way and cheering her on. I think she has indeed changed in many ways since her stay in prison. How it all plays out is guaranteed to be very interesting.

I continue to visit with those in Martha's family I am closest to: her daughter, Alexis, her brother George, and her sister Laura. They all still have their complicated relationships to work out with Martha, just like every family. I check in with Martha, and her niece Sophie also is dear to my heart. Martha stays busy but always has time for close friends. I am happy to be among them.

"There's only one Martha," says her mother. "No one can duplicate what she did. She must have been at the right place at the right time for her to assume all this importance in people's lives. People come up to me and strangers write me about how much she has influenced them and how much they love her. She's touched a lot of people. She didn't start out to do it; it just got bigger and bigger. Martha is a teacher. She has taught people to do many things and not in the way an ordinary teacher would, but in her own particular way. She taught people about the good things in life—the simple things—and then those things became very important after she brought them into view."

Lexi says, "Nothing my mother has shown the world can do any harm. Don't we all want a better life? No matter what they say about my mom, all she ever does is teach the world good things that will help them in life. So what if she shows you the perfect way to do it? She's not showing off. Would you want your professor at school to do anything less in any other subject? So what if she aspires to do everything perfectly? Don't we all try to do that? At least most of us do. Why tear her down for that? Go tear down the porn kings or the fast-food chains or other people who feed trash to your children. My mom has never spoken a bad word about anyone who has talked unkindly about her. I know that for sure."

Eva Scrivo says, "Maybe some people are jealous of her vision. Martha felt it was enriching to experience and to learn the good things, and she taught as a natural extension of that. Her teaching is really about how delicious all the experiences of life are. I think Martha is somewhat of a young girl at heart. She always says, 'Look at that; oh my God, isn't that *amazing*?' She doesn't just stand there by herself to appreciate things—she shares what she sees with the rest of us."

Millions have shared Martha's vision and have been pulled into her charismatic aura and her world. I feel this pull myself whenever I see her on television or in person, and I surrender willingly.

Lexi is enjoying her new life in her mother's world. "I actually like my new position at *Martha Stewart Living*," she said as she sliced big wedges of rich yellow cake and handed me a fork. "My mother and I are working side by side and it's something she's wanted for a long time. She's overcome a huge obstacle and she's moving forward. We both are."

Lexi and I sat down to dig into the warm cake. It was incredibly delicious.

Epilogue:
Martha
Triumphant

Martha knows more than most of us that it's all about courage. Her ankle bracelet came off in early September 2005, and there was no keeping the force of Martha contained or enclosed after that.

Suddenly she is everywhere. I snuggled into the breakfast nook at home with a big mug of coffee to watch the premiere episode of *Martha*. And there she was—boom! Back on television as if she hadn't missed a beat. I loved the relaxed interaction between Martha and the audience. This is the Martha I know—down-to-earth, fun, and laughing with the best of them. The next day, I nearly fell off my chair when I saw her whip up snacks in the microwave using recipes she'd learned in prison. She was showing her new jail hors d'oeuvres to the former *Saturday Night Live* comedian David Spade, who teased her mercilessly about her incarceration. Martha took it all in good humor.

I wasn't surprised when the show got the best ratings she has ever had—beating the success of *Martha Stewart Living*.

Half the time the audience members are among the stars of the show. They've brought their ponchos, their family recipes, and their show-and-tell items. Martha's fans are connecting with her more vulnerable, human side.

On the premiere of *The Apprentice: Martha Stewart* a week later, Martha showed the side of her that is a kinder, gentler boss. The contestants ate off beautiful Martha Stewart plates and slept on Martha Stewart sheets from Kmart. When she had to fire one of them in the show-no-mercy tradition of her friend Donald Trump, she instead let the poor soul down nicely, saying "You just don't fit in." Then she wrote a cordial note to the fired contestant in her precise handwriting—no doubt on the special stationery I have seen so often in our correspondence over the years. I guess after all these years Martha has finally learned to apologize.

Martha's family is proud as they can be. Lexi was sitting in the audience for the first episode of *Martha*, and Mrs. Kostyra watched on the TV at Turkey Hill with Martha's housekeepers Lara and Odete, as they all sipped their morning tea. The whole family watched from wherever they were.

The show Mrs. Kostyra had told me about in July turned out to be a ninety-first birthday celebration that Martha hosted in honor of her mother. Martha and the chef John Baricelli made Mrs. Kostyra's favorite, a rich and delicious carrot cake.

"Oh, look at Martha—she always looks so good on camera. She's got those long, thin legs," one family member said to me while watching as *Martha* aired. "Our Martha . . . she's back in the saddle."

Martha is a really fun show, both instructive and entertaining in the best tradition of *Martha Stewart Living*. Martha has a celebrity guest on the show every day, as well as lots of fun and useful how-to cooking and homekeeping segments. For Martha's Halloween show, the special guest was the soap opera star Cameron Mathison dressed as Tarzan; Martha dressed as Jane, and a good time was had by all.

Early one morning, Laura picked me up and we went into Manhattan to see a taping of *Martha* together. Backstage, the loyal Martha team was in high gear—her producer Lisa scurried about, and Eva Scrivo was close by, ready with her comb and scissors. Martha and I shared a big hug as the audience waited for her arrival. You could feel the excitement and energy in the air. When Martha finally stepped out in front of the cameras where she belonged, the fans in the studio went wild. It was as if she were a rock star. I thought to myself, with a sense of awe, *This is Martha Stewart—and she is no ordinary human being.*

"You know, Lloyd," Lexi told me once, "my mother is going to surprise the world once again. You can bet on that."

She already has. And I'm looking forward to all of Martha's good things in the many years to come.

Index